To Reeta,
   In appreciation In t
looking forward to co

D0408862

The Construction of a Political Community

The Construction of a Political Community
Integration and Identity in Goa

ARTHUR G RUBINOFF

SAGE PUBLICATIONS
New Delhi/Thousand Oaks/London

First published in 1998 by

Sage Publications India Pvt Ltd
M-32 Market Greater Kailash – I
New Delhi – 110 048

Sage Publications Inc
2455 Teller Road
Thousand Oaks, California 91320

Sage Publications Ltd
6 Bonhill Street
London EC2A 4PU

Published by Tejeshwar Singh for Sage Publications India Pvt Ltd, phototypeset by Pagewell Photosetters, Pondicherry and printed at Chaman Enterprises, Delhi.

Library of Congress Cataloging-in-Publication Data

Rubinoff, Arthur G., 1942–
    The construction of a political community : integration and identity in Goa / Arthur G. Rubinoff.
        p.   cm.   (alk. paper)
    Includes bibliographical references and index.
     1. Goa (India: State)—Politics and government.   I. Title.
  JQ620.G6A47   320.954'799—dc21   1998   98–7052

ISBN: 0–7619–9259–6 (US-HB)   81–7036–717–4 (India-HB)

Sage Production Team: Sasmita Sinha, M.S.V. Namboodiri and Santosh Rawat

For
Derek and Kailan
Who Shared the Experience

Contents

◆

List of Tables

◆

G O A

MAHARASHTRA

KARNATAKA

PERNEM

• Pernem

Chapora R.

BARDEZ

• Mapusa

• Bicholim

SATARI

BICHOLIM

• Valpoi

Mapuca R.

Mandovi R.

⊙ PANAJI

TISWADI

Marmagao •

• Ponda

Vasco-da-Gama

MARMAGAO

PONDA

SANGUEM

Zuvari R.

Sal R.

• Margao

Candeper R.

ARABIAN SEA

SALCETTE

Sanguem •

Sanguem R.

• Quepem

Paroda R.

QUEPEM

CANACONA

• Chauri

Talpona R.

Galgibaga R.

KEY

• MAJOR TOWNS

— TALUKA BOUNDARY

⊙ CAPITAL

INDIA

Preface and Acknowledgements

◆

This book is the product of over thirty years of research on Goa. I first began studying the politics of the former Portuguese possessions on the Indian subcontinent at the University of Chicago under the supervision of Lloyd Rudolph in 1965. A seminar paper evolved into my master's thesis on the military takeover of the Portuguese colonies. While taking a course on state politics in India, I discovered there was no literature that dealt with Goa since its incorporation into the Union. I recognized the need for such a study, but did my Ph.D. dissertation on 'India's Foreign Relations with Egypt and Yugoslavia'. A Fulbright Fellowship to India on that subject in 1968–69 enabled me to visit Goa for the first time. It was then that I decided to continue my research on Goa.

A sabbatical leave grant from the Social Sciences and Humanities Research Council of Canada during the 1978–79 academic year enabled me to begin fieldwork on political developments since 1961. Support from the Office of Research Administration of the University of Toronto allowed me to observe the 1979–80, 1991, 1996 and 1998 election campaigns. Research grants from South Asia Ontario in 1990 and the Shastri Indo–Canadian Institute in 1993–94 enabled me to briefly return to Goa to study the attainment of statehood. Most recently, assistance from the Smithsonian Institution administered by the American Institute of Indian Studies enabled me to do research on the 1994 and 1996 elections and complete the volume.

A revision of my master's thesis *India's Use of Force in Goa* was published by Popular Prakashan of Bombay in 1971. It examined the problem of Goa in the conflicting contexts of India's Gandhian commitment to the pacific settlement of international disputes and

New Delhi's desire to lead the anti-colonial struggle in the Afro-Asian world. External pressure from the Afro-Asian states ultimately led the government of Prime Minister Jawaharlal Nehru to use military force to expel the Portuguese in December 1961. In this present study of the integration of the former Portuguese colonies *since* 1961, I have tried not to repeat my earlier work. While some material overlaps, particularly in chapters 2 and 3, I have employed it in a comparative politics—as opposed to an international relations—framework. Moreover, I have updated my sources to take into account recently published documents and writings. A version of the chapter on integration theory appeared in *The Journal of Developing Societies* and the one on statehood was first published in *Asian Survey*. The 1996 election campaign was initially discussed in *Economic and Political Weekly*.

Over the past three decades I have interviewed hundreds of politicians, academics, businessmen, journalists, and government officials in connection with this study—many, more than once. I am particularly grateful to Froilano Machado, Pratapsingh Rane, and Ferdino Rebello, who allowed me to accompany them on their campaigns in 1979. Other former legislators like Vasant Joshi have been extremely kind. I am appreciative of the help I have had in Goa from friends like Govind Parvatker, who assisted with my research, and Kote Chandra Shaker, who helped in innumerable ways while I lived there. Similarly, I am indebted to the Mandovi Hotel in Panjim which always found room for me no matter what the season. I gratefully acknowledge the assistance provided by librarians in the Home Ministry and the National Council of Applied Economic Research in New Delhi, Bombay University, the Central Library of Panjim, Delhi University, and especially A.B. Ulam, secretary of the Legislative Assembly of Goa, and his under secretary, Y.S. Amonkar who made available transcripts of unpublished debates. No one has been more helpful to me in the conduct of my work in India than Prem Nath Malik, the administrative director of the Shastri Indo– Canadian Institute, who looks after me when I am in his country. I appreciate the manner in which Sage India handled my manuscript. I would like to thank Omita Goyal, the acquisitions editor, for her interest in the project, and Sasmita Sinha for her careful copy editing.

A number of scholars have contributed to my thinking on this project: commentators on papers I have presented at academic conferences, like Rod Church, John Wood, Hari Sharma, and T.V. Paul; anonymous referees and editors of journals to whom I have submitted manuscripts, especially Leo Rose. Many colleagues including Henry Benin, Ron Manzer, Lloyd Rudolph and most significantly Victor Falkenheim have commented on various versions of this work. All deserve my thanks. No one has contributed more to my study of Goa for thirty-three years than my wife Janet, herself an expert on Goan culture and society. I am grateful for her expertise, constructive criticism, and editorial talent.

I dedicate this volume to my children, Derek and Kailan, who were respectively eight and four when they accompanied me to Goa. Although to their bewilderment, as Europeans, they were first called 'hippies' when they enrolled in school, they soon became Goans.

Chapter 1

Political Integration in the Indian States

◆

As Myron Weiner observed in a seminal study, 'There are few problems in political development in other countries not found in some form within the Indian states and no problems of development within the Indian states not found outside of India' (Weiner 1968: 18). Given India's federal structure, patterns of development within its constituent entities are crucial to an understanding of the country's political system. Each of the Indian states provides an unusual microcosm and macrocosm for studying processes of development: a microcosm since the states are units of a larger system, and a macrocosm since the units may be studied as separate political systems (ibid.: 4). Although the units of India's federal system share a common legal–constitutional framework as well as administrative structures, their internal political patterns vary considerably since each state has undergone its own sequence of political development in its own social and economic environment.

The politics of Goa are illustrative of the all-India problems of administrative development and the process of integrating diverse social, linguistic, and religious groups. However, they also reflect the region's uniqueness: the result of 450 years of Portuguese, rather than three centuries of exposure to British, colonialism—a condition that resulted in a lack of roots for both democratic institutions and the Congress party. Unlike the situation in British India where Congress politicians gained valuable legislative experience in the period 1937–39, the establishment of meaningful politics in Goa came only after its incorporation into the Indian Union in December 1961. For two decades after its liberation the Congress, because of its lack of historical roots in Goa, was repeatedly unable to achieve electoral success in a communal setting. Its ideology of secularism clashed with existing primordial loyalties.

Goa's unique colonial, cultural, ethnic, and linguistic heritage and its relatively recent incorporation into the Indian Union make the area an important case-study for the application of integration theory. In an era when multinational states such as Czechoslovakia, the Soviet Union, and Yugoslavia have disintegrated and others like Spain and Canada are under stress from separatist movements, the integrity of the Indian Union is also threatened. At the time of Goa's territorial annexation, the locus of its population's emotional identity was unknown. Yet, in contrast to other parts of the country (see Mitra and Lewis 1996), national identity in Goa has been enhanced.

Goa's post-colonial democratic integration will serve as a significant basis of comparison with the experience of other European enclaves in the developing world. Their fate has attracted more concern in Great Britain and the United States than did Goa's incorporation into India. India's use of force in Goa has made Lisbon more willing to negotiate a diplomatic solution with China over Macao—something it refused to do with New Delhi. Goa, a former colony of fascist Portugal, was transformed by the democratic state of India, while Hong Kong and Macao are being taken over by a communist regime. As China absorbs Hong Kong and Macao, Goa's ability to develop in a democratic context may well prove to underscore the unusualness of the Indian path of integration. Certainly the evolution of Goan society and politics within India can be contrasted with the fate of Portugal's former African possessions which have continued to repress democratic freedoms.

This book is an examination of New Delhi's attempts to promote nationalist sentiment in Goa since India's military forces territorially integrated the former Portuguese possession in December 1961. Since the Portuguese were more concerned with security considerations than promoting the development of their colonial holdings, political and economic progress could only follow territorial integration with India. As New Delhi was developing and integrating the subcontinent's former Portuguese colonies at a time India itself was being integrated into the world economy, its experience with Goa could be considered a case of double integration. Moreover, New Delhi had to overcome both British and Portuguese colonial legacies in integrating Goa. Although India has been successful in transplanting its democratic political system and promoting economic development in Goa, New Delhi, characteristically, has proceeded pragmatically rather than programmatically. As will be demonstrated, the centre has tended to respond to events in Goa rather than shape them.

After examining Goa's incorporation into the Indian Union, the study analyzes the problems of transition and the response of Goan ethnic and social groups to the process of integration which culminated on May 30, 1987 when Goa became India's twenty-fifth state. Initially, the task of integrating Goans into the country divided them. Yet, over time national politics emerged and the performance of the territorial government became more important than communal considerations in determining electoral behaviour.

The failure of both Catholic and Hindu Goans to struggle together in a mass nationalist movement created a leadership vacuum that politicians in other states attempted to fill. During the 1960s the non-Brahman Hindus promoted merger with Maharashtra. Their vehicle in this endeavour was the Maharashtrawadi Gomantak Party (MGP or MG). Although it claimed to be an integrating agent, by championing regional as opposed to national integration, the MGP's campaigns for merger with Maharashtra in fact exacerbated sectarian differences. However, the Opinion Poll in 1967 forced those Catholics who had gravitated to the United Goans Party (UGP or UG) in an attempt to resist the dilution of their community's distinct culture, to cooperate with the nationalist Hindu Brahmans who traditionally supported the Congress. In the process of rejecting merger with Maharashtra, Goans solidified their identity. Following the failure of the merger campaign, it became permissible for Hindu Goans to emphasize their local identity by voting for the regional party and against the Congress. As a result of their minority position in the territory, it was the Goan Christians who pursued integration into the larger Indian Union in the form of statehood. What is unique in the Goan case is that it was the minority Christian community that risked bloodshed by taking the initiative in campaigning for statehood. As was the situation during the 1967 Opinion Poll, the Christians made common cause with the Hindu Brahman community in order to advance the Konkani language. Earlier research on the pattern of post-liberation politics in Goa supported the findings of those social scientists who believe that while the introduction of democratic

National Conference *✗*

politics initially causes issus to be expressed in communal terms, such sectarian conflict eventually generates political parties and other institutions that penetrate the body politic and facilitate national integration. However, the manner in which Goa achieved statehood suggests that Indian politicians are not averse to reviving communal issues such as language, in order to promote selfish objectives. As a way of gaining political support for their own personal agendas, they pose issues in cultural terms, like the promotion of the Konkani language.

The book concludes with an assessment of the impact that integration with India has had on transforming the former Portuguese territories on the subcontinent. It finds that while economic development has fostered integration with India, it has eroded the area's distinctive identity. In contrast to other parts of the country, politics in Goa have become more national because of the demographic changes brought about by both in and out migration and the fact that an entire generation has come of age under Indian rule. Thus Goans—as well as Goa—have been transformed by the process of their integration with the Indian Union.

The Process of Integration

Political integration is a process whereby actors from distinct systems or pre-existing subsystems are expected to shift their loyalties, expectations, and political activities towards a new centre whose institutions demand or possess jurisdiction over the pre-existing units (Haas 1968: 16). Fundamental to the concept is the transformation of previously separate units into components of a coherent system by addition or combination (Zolberg 1967: 449). Integration may be defined as 'the degree of cohesion that binds members of social systems together, and is generally thought of in terms of values, institutions and communications which facilitate escalating sequences of social contact, cooperation and consensus' (Morrison and Stevenson 1972b: 903). For Myron Weiner, it entails the process of bringing culturally and socially discrete groups into a single territorial unit; the establishment of a national identity; the imposition of central authority over subordinate political units; linking the government with the governed; and the promotion of common values through political socialization so that the authorities can maintain order and carry out programmatic goals (Weiner

Integration

1965: 53–54). The principal actor in the process of creating a new identity becomes the fledgling state (Brass 1985: 8).

Although the term has been employed by social scientists since the nineteenth century, it is only relatively recently that integration of non-homogeneous states has become an issue for political scientists. Historically students of nationalism were preoccupied with describing the phenomenon's ideological nature in Europe (see Stokes 1978), but were not concerned with the question of national loyalties in Asia and Africa. Hence, from the middle of the last century, most social theorists believed that the development of industrial society would lead to the disappearance of conflicts based on ethnic or cultural divisions (Birch 1978: 325). While Marxists assumed that such conflicts were a passing phase that would be superseded by the class struggles of industrial society, American advocates of the 'melting pot' ideal of assimilation viewed ethnic divisions as residual loyalties that were the product of an earlier phase of social development (Waldron 1985).

It is the polyethnic character of the dozens of new states which have attained independence in the postwar era that caused political integration to be viewed as a significant issue. The initial literature of the post-colonial period addressed the subject from the perspective of state-building, since the process was occurring simultaneously with nation-building (see Phadnis 1989: 25). As nationalism has tended to be legitimated by statehood, the problem for the new states is one of contending ethnic claims (Smith 1981). Ethnic groups demand and bargain for collective entitlements that have to be refereed by a state apparatus (Tambiah 1996: 16). The combination of new economic and political relationships and existing traditional loyalties places great strains on ethnic groups and the fragile state which purports to represent the common (secular) as opposed to the special (communal) interest (J. Rothchild 1981). National leaders regarded the consciousness mobilized by the anti-colonial movement as the antithesis of communalism which they regarded as 'nationalism gone awry.'[1] Accordingly, for them state-formation was associated with nation-formation, where the government would play a decisive role in the construction of a new political community that would address issues that had been neglected by the colonial regime (Tremblay 1997). Indeed, as Stanley Tambiah (1996: 15) points out, Jawaharlal Nehru in his autobiography and popular book *The Discovery of India*, 'eloquently preached the promise of

Indian nationalism and cultural renaissance wedded to the organizing institution of the state, a marriage that would deliver social justice, economic growth, and scientific progress.'

Incorporation into a new political order triggers a radical shift in social circumstances that is the hallmark of ethnic change (Keyes 1981). Cynthia Enloe (1973: 15) believes 'as social relations become more complex and impersonal, ethnic identity may be grasped tenaciously' because it 'is a familiar and reassuring anchor in a climate of turbulence and uncertainty.' The expansion of the political process and the extension of governmental activity in the post-colonial states aggravate tensions between competing groups (Binder 1964). As Myron Weiner observed about the process of integration, the scale and volume of conflict between social groups increases as societies modernize. Communities 'once low in status and wealth, may now rise or at least see the opportunity for mobility,' while 'social groups once high in power, status and wealth may now feel threatened.' As a result, 'traditional rivalries are aggravated, and new conflicts are created as social relationships change' (Weiner 1965: 59). As will become evident, this is exactly what happened in the case of Goa.

As most states have within arbitrary post-colonial borders at least five ethnically disparate groups (Lambert 1977), their integration has become one of the salient tasks of nation-building (see van den Helm 1974). Claude Ake (1967: 1) has characterized it as the 'crucial problem of the post-colonial situation.' How to accommodate conflicting demands of regional groups while at the same time fostering national unity has long been a problem for policy-makers. The resolution of such conflicts is essential, since the outcome can be either deeper integration or continued hostility that may lead to national disintegration (Mazuri 1969: 335). When a fledgling central authority strives to create civil sentiments consistent with nationalism, it faces resistance to competing primordial sentiments whether they be labelled tribalism, communalism, or merely parochialism (Geertz 1963: 111).

As Donald L. Horowitz (1985: xii–xiii) demonstrates in his comprehensive comparative study, 'Ethnicity is one of those forces that is community–building in moderation and community–destroying in excess.' The outcome in any given situation depends on whether traditional groups are capable of meeting the needs for personal identity, social welfare, and economic advancement which are weakened by the ensuing social transformation. Whether or not the imposition of central authority leads the citizen of a new state to refocus his identity is a matter of dispute. At least two schools of thought, advancing conflicting assumptions, have arisen in the literature concerning the relationship of nationalism to political integration: 'one which views nationalism as a process of successive integration of social groups and another which views nationalism as a process of conflicting relations among social groups' (Hah and Martin 1975: 361). On the one hand, Karl Deutsch (1953a; 1953b; 1961) finds assimilation to be the end result of such forms of social mobilization as urbanization, industrialization, increased mobility and other breakdowns of traditional geographic, social and primordial ties. On the other hand, the processes of modernization[2] can clearly exert disintegrative as well as integrative effects upon people. Walker Connor (1967; 1973) maintains fragmentation is the likely outcome of such a process. This is especially held to be the case when 'the crises of development come all at once, overwhelming the economic and social systems as well as the political system' (Scott 1966: 334). Advances in communications and transportation tend to increase the cultural awareness of groups by making their members more conscious of distinctions between themselves and others (Connor 1972: 329).

As Joseph LaPalombara and Myron Weiner (1966) point out, there are two ways regimes have of coping with such social diversity: One way is to employ force in order to eradicate it, while the other is to create institutional arrangements that encourage dialogue and facilitate the articulation and aggregation of conflicting interests so that national unity may be constructed out of ethnic diversity. These two methods of conflict regulation advanced by cultural pluralists are the consociational and control approaches, and both are deemed applicable to deeply segmented societies. (On this point see Lustick 1979; and Kasfir 1979.) The consociational approach differs from other theories of integration by asserting that cultural cleavages induce conflict resolution not fragmentation (Lijphart 1971: 11). In such a situation of accommodation, the elites must have the ability and desire to transcend cleavages in order to promote cohesion and stability among the various subcultures of the political system (Lijphart 1969: 216). However, critics of the consociational model, such as Brian Barry (1975a; 1975b; cf. Daalder 1974), caution that manipulative techniques that elite cartels employ in an effort to maintain stability can aggravate rather than ameliorate segmented conflict. Indeed, as Eric Nordlinger (1972: 31) has shown, the stronger elements of a political community often employ federal arrangements as a device to dominate weaker sectors.

Whether the solution pursued by any country is the promotion of assimilation or the acceptance of cultural pluralism, demands are made on the respective minority and majority communities (Esman 1977). On the one hand, assimilation demands that the minorities consent to abandon their distinguishing ethnic, cultural, and linguistic characteristics and become combined with majorities with whom they live in nationally uniform communities. It also requires that the majorities concerned accept and facilitate this merger. Cultural pluralism, on the other hand, requires that majorities respect the peculiar characteristics of minorities and foster their development. For their part, minorities must accept the obligation of being temperate in their demands for autonomy. In Inis Claude's words, 'In the one case, minorities are expected to relinquish their insistence on being different; in the other, majorities are expected to abandon their intolerance of those who are different' (1955: 79).

In culturally pluralistic societies like India, loyalties, mobilization, and conflict tend to be expressed in communal terms where group solidarities are based on shared caste, ethnic, linguistic, racial, regional or religious identities (Anderson et al. 1974: 17). In some cases these loyalties rival or exceed those which the state is able to generate. However, the stability of culturally plural societies is usually threatened not by communalism per se, but by the failure of national institutions explicitly to recognize and accommodate existing communal divisions and interests (Melson and Wolpe 1970: 1114). Thus, regimes which are committed to pluralism accord legitimacy to identities and solidarities, permit communal groups to organize and articulate their cultural and political interests, and attempt to cope with the inevitable competition and conflict primarily by structured bargaining processes (Esman 1973: 60).

Since political organizations and secondary associations tend to organize on a communal basis in societies characterized by segmental cleavages (Lorwin 1971: 141), political, ethnonational, and regional conflicts are more intense than those generated in societies where disagreement is focused around specific policy issues (Zuckerman 1975: 235; Tambiah 1996). Cleavages within the new states are often fundamental in nature rendering domestic inter-group relations akin to those which prevail in the international system (Roth-child 1970: 597). As these disputes are often legacies of arbitrary colonial borders which have divided ethnic groups, they often spill over international boundaries and blur the distinction between interstate and intrastate conflicts. Typified by situations like Rwanda, such conflicts have resulted in the deaths of twenty million people and created an equal number of refugees since World War II (Welsh 1993: 63). Although few new countries were created because of ethnic secession in the first forty years after World War II, the importance of integration is once again highlighted by the resurgence of ethnonationalism depicted in the break-up of the multi-ethnic polities of Eastern Europe and the devolution of power in the established states of Western Europe (Smith 1993). While only the special cases of Singapore and Bangladesh were created in the first forty years of the cold war, since 1991 at least eighteen new national states have been recognized on the principle of ethnic secession (Smith 1995: 104). The fact that India is also a country of disparate nationalities is reason enough for New Delhi to view these developments with alarm.

The Indian Situation

Due to the country's diverse religious, linguistic and social com-position, the task of integration has been especially crucial and difficult for India (see Mason 1967; Elder 1964), which contains within its boundaries virtually 'every form of cultural challenge to civil politics' (Young 1976: 274). The various stratifications provide the 'raw material for a huge number of possible identities' (Taylor 1979: 257). While the resulting cleavages have led to predictions of national disintegration (see especially Harrison 1960), India's extreme pluralism may also be viewed 'as one of the strengths of the Indian polyarchy [since it] compels the leaders of every group to learn and practice the arts of conciliation and coalition formation and prevents any single unified group from even approaching a monopoly of political resources' (Dahl 1971: 117–18). On balance, India's efforts—particularly in the context of the size and diversity of the country—may be regarded as one of the more successful attempts at nation-building by a new state (Srinivas 1976: 11; for a more technical view see Kahane 1982). As Francine Frankel (1978: 20) put it, the entire political structure was built upon accommodating existing linguistic, religious and caste sentiments 'as the only way to accelerate national integration, enhance the legitimacy of the political system, and maximize the possibility of peaceful adjustments of social conflicts that arise during the development process.' Hence, unlike the situation in other countries (see Smith 1991: 133), India's post-colonial state has not suffered from a fragile legitimacy.

As Atul Kohli (1997: 344) observes, 'democracy in a developing-country setting both encourages ethnic conflict and, under specific circumstances, provides a framework for their accommodation.' The Indian formula for promoting national integration has been to reconcile culturally pluralistic demands through a democratic political system in such a way that the end product is 'a reasonable politico-economic deal rather than secession from the national mainstream' (Narain 1976: 903). In India 'the weakening of traditional authority and cohesiveness has been accompanied not by the disappearance of communal identities but by their transformation and expansion' (Melson and Wolpe 1970: 1130). Jyotirindra Das Gupta (1970) maintains that while politics between groups in segmented societies like India are initially conducted on a communal basis, they eventually lead to the creation of interest groups, political parties and other institutions that penetrate the body politic and in the long run promote integration. The Rudolphs (1967) have similarly demonstrated the adaptability of traditional Indian institutions.

Thus, despite claims to the contrary (Morrison and Stevenson 1972a: 88), the Indian experience suggests that cultural homogeneity is not a requisite for either political integration or democratic stability. The contrasting experiences of India and Sri Lanka indicate that the larger the number of ethnic groups included in the political process, the smaller the consequences any one communal dispute has for the stability of the entire political system (Manor 1982). As Seymour Martin Lipset (1963: 14) noted, 'the chances for stable democracy are enhanced to the extent that groups and individuals have a number of crosscutting, politically relevant affiliations.' Hence, political and cultural divisions do not necessarily hinder political integration in countries like India (Das Gupta 1968: 20).

The prospects for the establishment of democratic pluralism in any country are improved to the extent that there is a consensus on values and the procedural norms of government (van de Berghe 1969: 76). As Crawford Young (1976: 314) suggests, the type of bargaining–pressure politics found in India has a great deal in common with Arend Lijphart's theory of consociational democracy developed for the Netherlands and other Western European countries. Although Lijphart (1968; see also McCrae 1974) initially maintained that India's size militates his scheme's applicability, he later (1996) confirmed[3] that it meets his requirements that elites possess a common perception of interests as well as the ability and desire to accommodate the various subcultures of the political system (Lijphart 1977: 225 and 168; and 1969). In the first two decades after independence, India's elite—whether party leaders, intellectuals or bureaucrats—shared a remarkable degree of common political socialization that produced a politics based on reconciliation. It was during this period that Goa was incorporated into the country.

In India the principal mechanism for the resolution of political disputes and the regulation of social conflict has been the dominant Congress party (see Kothari 1964; Kochanek 1968; and Weiner 1967 for an elaboration of conflict resolution procedures). Nevertheless, when presented an opportunity to aggrandize their respective power and influence, political parties have tended to give more consideration to local and regional demands than to the needs and requirements of the nation as a whole (Chandra, et al. 1976: 1). Indeed, regional parties such as the Akali Dal in Punjab and the DMK in Tamil Nadu have enjoyed success by advancing communal concerns to the point of threatening separation.[4] In addition, all-India parties such as the communists have tended to advocate political and linguistic decentralization because their support tends to be regionally based. (On this point see Overstreet and Windmiller 1959.) More often than not, even the Congress has succumbed to state and regional pressures when faced with electoral setbacks (see Stern 1970). Hence, despite the admitted reservations of Prime Minister Jawaharlal Nehru, who feared the emergence of embryonic subnationalism (see Harrison 1956), the linguistic state formula was embraced by the *Report of the States Reorganization Commission* in 1955 (Chapter 3). Federalism reinforces pluralism by shaping group identities within a multi-cultural society. The problem for the system is the difficulty of maintaining an egalitarian society when leaders attempt to mobilize votes on the basis of primordial loyalties and distribute benefits to narrowly-based constituencies (Tremblay 1997). Nevertheless, after assessing the historical experience of the decentralization associated with states' reorganization, one thoughtful analyst of Indian politics has concluded, it not only 'provided the framework for expanded participation [but] made the people more accessible to political mobilization, and at the same time provided them with increased institutional access for the articulation of demands' (Hardgrave 1970: 90).

While some like Gyanendra Pandey (1990: viii) view the term 'communalism' as 'loaded and obfuscating,' India is understandably sensitive to the issue of religious strife because of the partition in 1947 which resulted in an unparalleled transfer of population with Pakistan. (An excellent treatment of this inheritance is provided by Brown 1972.) It still leaves as its legacy destabilizing patterns of migration and local resistance to outsiders (see Weiner 1978) and the ongoing separatist rebellions in the northeast. This concern has been heightened in recent years by the campaign for independence waged by Sikh advocates of Khalistan in the Punjab since the 1980s and the civil war conducted by Muslim separatists in Kashmir during this decade (Hardgrave 1993). In addition to the process of integrating its multiplicity of ethnic nationalities, India also underwent the post-independence task of absorbing 574 princely states (see Menon 1961). In the 1960s, the Government of India established a National Integration Council under the chairmanship of the prime minister and has from time to time convened National Integration Conferences in order to combat communalism, caste-ism, lingualism, regionalism, and other forms of parochialism by providing economic opportunities for minorities and promoting a national outlook in the field of education.[5]

As will be seen, the Congress party's inability to act as an integrating agent in the face of communal challenges began in Goa, the one area in India where it had no roots. Since 1967 the Congress party's ability to ameliorate social conflict in the rest of the country has been in decline (see Kohli 1990). The emergence of less sophisticated vernacular politicians who play the communal card has contributed to the breakdown of the earlier elite consensus and consociational style of politics. Secularism's viability and credibility are dependent on the state's ability to be regarded as neutral (Pandey 1993: 3–4). When a political community's authorities are perceived by the populace as corrupt politicians who act in the selfish rather than the public interest, the state and its agents lose their legitimacy. While the institutions of India's secular constitution and representative system of government were predicated on the protection of the individual rights of its citizens, collectives in the form of ethnic groups and *jatis*, seeking preferences in the name of equality have become the country's principal political actors (Tambiah 1996: 335). As Peter van der Veer (1994: 23) asserts, there is a considerable gap between the Indian state's pluralist pretensions and its actual functioning that produces violence. Religious and caste conflicts have been endemic in the decade of the 1990s as the state attempts to accommodate its backward communities. Violent sectarian divisiveness followed the implementation of the Mandal Commission Report in 1990. It caused India's majority Hindus to stress their distinctive caste identities in order to obtain reservations in educational institutions and government jobs. These disturbances, which were followed by renewed Hindu–Muslim strife exemplified by the ethno-religious disturbances in Ayodhya and Bombay (see Varshney 1993; Jaffrelot 1996), have undermined the public's confidence in the ability of the state to be a neutral actor capable of fairly distributing resources and providing order in civil society (Brass 1997).

Due to its continuing commitment to national integration at a time of increasing civil strife, New Delhi has not been anxious to take measures which might promote parochial identities at the periphery in places like Goa. Whether ethnic politics is considered 'more parochial or more central is mainly a function of group size to state size' (Horowitz 1971: 239). As Paul Brass (1994: 7) has asserted, New Delhi has followed 'two strict rules' in dealing with ethnic, religious, linguistic and cultural group demands: 'The first is that no secessionist movement will be entertained and that any group which takes up a secessionist stance will, while it is weak, be ignored and treated as illegitimate,' but, second, should it develop significant strength a rebellion 'will be smashed, with armed force if necessary.' With respect to other parts of India, Brass (1974: 17–18) has demonstrated that regional demands based on culture and language are not conceded capriciously by the Union Government—especially when the territorial unit is as small as Goa.

END NOTES

1. Pandey (1990: 14) associates this view with Chandra (1984: 125–27).
2. Jacob and Toscano (1964) list ten: (1) geographical proximity; (2) homogeneity; (3) transactions or interactions among persons or groups; (4) knowledge of each other; (5) shared functional interests; (6) the 'character' or motive pattern of a group; (7) the structural frame or system of power and decision-making; (8) the sovereignty–dependency status of the community; (9) governmental effectiveness; (10) previous governmental experience.
3. Ironically, Lijphart's belated recognition that consociationalism applied to India occurred after mechanisms for confronting and adjudicating disputes had already broken down.
4. For relevant discussions of politics in these states during this period see Raj Nayar (1966), Brass (1975), Barnett (1976), and Hardgrave (1965).
5. These objectives were outlined in the publication *National Integration* in 1961.

Chapter 2

Patterns of Integration Between Goa and India Before 1961

◆

Goan Identity

As Stanley Tambiah (1996: 20) suggests, ethnic identity is above all self-proclaimed collective identity. For Anthony Smith it starts from 'a recognisable cultural unit' whose 'primary concern' is 'to ensure the survival of the group's *cultural* identity' (Smith 1971: 216–17). Identity can be based on such attributes as skin colour, language, religion, common descent, territorial occupation or mytho-historical legacy, or it can, in the case of an ethnic collectivity, be an imagined community in the terminology of Benedict Anderson (1983) that exists largely in the minds of its believers (Cohen 1985: 109). If a community is defined as a group of people who, in identifying with one another, have certain attitudes and beliefs in common and differentiate themselves from groups that lack these sentiments or qualities (Cassinelli 1969: 16), then the Goans certainly qualify for such a designation. As a cultural group rooted in Goan soil, and sharing the same set of traditions, all Goans, whether they be Hindus, Christians, or Muslims, recognize a common oneness that distinguishes them from others on the Indian subcontinent (Montemayor 1970: 447).

Whether or not ethnic groups conscious of their identity become politicized on that basis depends upon their degree of well-being or alienation from the rest of the political community (Brass 1976: 226), and the ability of elites to organize and make political demands (Brass 1991: 41). These demands, which the state must address, 'generally center on territory, resources, and power' (Basu 1997:

mobilization slow

396). As will be seen, such mobilization was slow in forthcoming in Goa and so was the response of the Government of India.

Portuguese Rule

Goa's political insularity from the rest of India stems from the condition that the European power which occupied the colony in A.D. 1510 was Portugal. Prior to its political and territorial separation by the Portuguese, the Goan enclave had been integrated within the political and cultural system of the medieval Hindu and Muslim kingdoms of the Konkan region. Over the next 450 years a distinctive Indo-Portuguese synthesis—or Lusitanian culture—was forged from the interaction between colonial and indigenous societies (see J. Rubinoff 1992). The long period of Portuguese occupation, as well as the colony's small territorial size (sixty miles long and forty miles wide), ensured that the Portuguese cultural impact was more concentrated than its British counterpart elsewhere on the Indian subcontinent. Yet, because of the autocratic nature of Portuguese rule, which included the creation of communal divisions based on religion (on this point see van der Veer 1994), it was less enduring.

Conquest

Sailing around Africa's Cape of Good Hope in search of commercial profits in the late fifteenth century, Portuguese navigators like Vasco da Gama traded on the Malabar coast of western India. The Portuguese who followed them embarked on a bitter struggle to wrest commercial advantage from the Muslims who dominated the area's trade. Their most famous explorer, Alfonso de Albuquerque erected forts at the site of spice factories he established.

The Goan territories on the Indian subcontinent were originally conquered from the Bijapur sultanate by Albuquerque, as part of Portugal's attempt to establish strategic points for commercial purposes on the west coast of India.[1] The acquisition provided an important link between Lisbon's African colonies and its possessions in the Southeast Asian spice islands. In the sixteenth and seventeenth centuries the island city and fortress of Goa were important bases in Portugal's competition with its European rivals on the subcontinent (see Lach 1968; Subrahmanyam 1993).

Albuquerque and his successors attempted to coerce the indigenous peoples into recognizing Portuguese suzerainty, but managed only to evoke bitter resistance from them—especially the Muslims. To obtain Rome's sanction over newly discovered lands, Lisbon, in accordance with the Papal Bull of Pope Alexander VI issued in 1493, pledged to propagate the faith in conquered territories. Under the terms of the *Padroado* with the Catholic Church, the state was responsible for the spread of Christianity (see Moraes 1964). Accordingly, Portugal embarked on a policy of forced conversions and the destruction of Hindu temples and Muslim mosques. In western India the Portuguese method of converting the inhabitants was to encourage their troops to marry the widows of slain Muslim soldiers. Besides playing off the Muslim and Hindu kingdoms against each other and destroying their houses of worship, the Portuguese in 1560 established an Inquisition in Goa (see Priolkar 1961; Higgs 1995). Although the Inquisition tapered off in the nineteenth century, it lasted until 1814.

As a consequence of these severe measures, neither the Catholic Church nor the Portuguese made much headway among the vast majority of Indians. The attempt to coerce people of the neighbouring areas into recognizing Portuguese suzerainty encountered fierce resistance from the Marathas (see Pisurlekar 1975). Competition from the Dutch and the British in the seventeenth century further curbed Portugal's attempts to expand its empire in Asia. With the assistance of the British, additional territories adjacent to Goa, known as the New Conquests, were added to the Portuguese holdings when there was a reorganization of the subcontinent by the European colonial powers during the period 1782–91. By that time the Portuguese Empire had been in decline for over a hundred years, and Lisbon had abandoned its intention to turn the Indian Ocean into a Portuguese lake. The Portuguese were able to retain their Indian footholds in the nineteenth century primarily because of the sympathetic cooperation of their British ally (see Pearson 1987; Cooper 1995). As a result of corruption and rapid deterioration, the Goan possessions that remained in Portuguese hands in the twentieth century were a lush but economically depressed colony that suffered from a shortage of foodstuffs and lacked adequate educational and transportation systems.[2]

Administration

Portuguese India evolved along similar administrative lines as the mother country. When the Portuguese monarchy was overthrown in 1910, there was a short interlude of liberalization before the fascist regime of Dr Antonio de Oliveira Salazar took control of the government in 1928. During the Republic the explicit discrimination practiced against Hindus was abolished, and persons of that faith could stand for elections and serve in the Portuguese parliament (Esteves 1986: 38). Lisbon's renewed neo-imperialistic sentiments were reflected in Article 2 of the Colonial Act promulgated in 1933 which read: 'It belongs to the organic essence of the Portuguese Nation to fulfill the historic mission of possessing and colonizing overseas dominions and of civilizing the native populations . . .' (quoted by Gaitonde and Mani 1956: 4). Lisbon was emphatic in professing that Goa was an integral part of Portugal and that its inhabitants were entitled to rights and privileges equal to those enjoyed by residents of the European part of the country.[3] As there was only one party on the ballot in fascist Portugal, with restrictions on association, suffrage, and civil liberties, Professor W.H. Morris-Jones (1954) characterized the exercise of these rights in Goa as not a 'very profound political experience.' The American Consulate General in Bombay in a dispatch to the secretary of state characterized the Portuguese administration in Goa as 'highly centralized and autocratic . . . comparable only to that existing in the prewar Nazi regime in Germany.'[4] The supreme head of the territories was the governor-general who was appointed by the Portuguese government. He served as the highest civil and military authority and the treasurer of the public exchequer. Until July 1955 he was assisted by a council of twelve members, of whom seven were officials nominated by the governor-general himself. At that time a new statute was introduced to meet the charge that the administration was dictatorial. It proclaimed Portuguese India to be an autonomous unit enjoying administrative decentralization. The act established a new council of twenty-two members, eleven of whom were elected on a direct basis, while the remainder were nominated by the government. Significantly, only 20,000 voters who were certified as 'politically acceptable' out of the 638,000 people who lived in the colony could qualify to select these eleven (P.K. Rao 1963: 49). Even after election, a member of the council was powerless to move a resolution without the prior consent of the governor-general. If the council were not in agreement with the governor-general, the latter could appeal to the overseas minister in Lisbon who held the power to reject the council's view. Thus, control over Goa remained in Lisbon and not in the hands of the indigenous population.

To ensure this domination, a rigid system of censorship was established. All printed matter, even wedding announcements, had to be read by the official censor. Illegal political activity was apt to be punished with either exile to Portugal or a long prison sentence or both. Under the circumstances, '. . . politics in Goa became a "hidden" activity carried on mainly by a few Goans in their individual or personal capacity in the territory or from outside Goa' (Esteves 1986: 47).

One consequence of Portuguese totalitarian measures was an extreme reluctance of the Goan people to talk freely about their political views. They remained an indeterminate quantity throughout the entire fourteen-year struggle between Portugal and India. Speculation about their feelings covered the entire spectrum from approval of Portuguese rule, preference for independence, and desire for annexation by India. Hence, one reporter could state, 'Goa belongs to Portugal only in name' (Glasgow 1954: 250), while Robert Trumbell of the *New York Times* claimed, 'On the whole, Goa appears to be a happier place in which to live than most of the subcontinent with less dissatisfaction than what has come to be considered normal in the greater part of India.'[5]

In 1951, in response to pressure by Indian nationalists, Portugal stopped referring to Goa as a colony. After that date Lisbon claimed that Goa and its other territories were overseas provinces, and thereby an integral part of metropolitan Portugal. There was no longer any pretense that these possessions would be developed towards eventual independence. By the mid-1950s Lisbon's quest for national destiny had degenerated into a frantic effort to retain its colonies.

Geography and Population

By 1954 about 1,500 square miles of India with a population of 638,000 remained under Portuguese control. These Portuguese territories were divided into three main districts—Goa, Daman, and Diu (see Parker 1955). Located on India's west coast, 250 miles (400 kilometres) south-southeast of Bombay, Goa had an area of 1,301 square miles—an area about the size of Rhode Island—and a population of 548,000. Situated on a parcel of land, 105 kilometres long and 60 kilometres wide between the Arabian Sea and the mountainous *Ghats*, its borders conformed to the region's geographical features. The territory's boundaries were defined in the north by the Tiracol river which separated it from Maharashtra in the north and hills which bordered Karnataka in the east. Goa was subdivided into eleven administrative units or *talukas*: Pernem, Bicholim, Satari, Bardez, Tiswadi (which includes the island of Goa known as *Ilhas* in Portuguese) in the north, and Ponda, Mormugao, Salcette, Sanguem, Quepem, and Canacon in the south. Daman, which had been captured by the Portuguese in 1559, consisted of three enclaves in Gujarat state, 100 miles north of Bombay. Its 214 square miles contained a population of 69,000, with 40,500 people residing in the two enclaves of Nagar Haveli and Dadra which were separated by a narrow strip of Indian territory. Diu, an island of twenty square miles with a population of 21,000 located off the coast of the Kathiawar peninsula north of Daman was conquered in 1546. Collectively these territories were called Goa and their principal city Panjim was designated the capital of Portuguese India.

The vast majority of Goans were linked racially, culturally, and linguistically to the inhabitants of the Indian Union which had received its independence from the British in 1947. One survey found that 86.4 per cent of the population had relations in India, while only 8.1 per cent had relations in Portuguese territories (Saksena 1974: 16). Racially, nearly all, or 636,153 persons, were of Indian stock. While many Goans had Portuguese surnames, this circumstance resulted from the fact that they took Christian names on conversion, not because they were descendants of Portuguese settlers (see J. Rubinoff 1995). The social structure of the Christian community is hierarchical along Hindu lines because converts carried their caste differences into their adopted religion. In the 1950s, 388,488 or 60.9 per cent of the residents of Goa were Hindus; 234,292 or 36.8 per cent were Christians, nearly all of these being Catholics residing in the coastal section of the Old Conquests which included the *talukas* of Bardez, Tiswadi, Mormugao, and Salcette; and 14,162 or 2.2 per cent were Muslims (J. Nehru 1956: 29). Konkani, a language closely related to Marathi, was declared by 95.8 per cent of the people to be their native tongue,[6] although Catholics employed Roman script and Hindus preferred Devanagari. In Daman and Diu, Gujarati was the principal language. Lisbon's failure to assimilate the Goans was reflected in the fact that only three per cent of the people spoke or understood Portuguese, the official language of the colonies.

Economy

Economically, Goa was linked more to India than to Portugal (see Lobo 1927). To some extent this was a reflection of geography for Goa was connected by road and rail to India, while Portugal in the 1950s could only be reached by ship and an air service that ran via Karachi. In any event, Goa exported very little to Portugal, as trade with the mother country amounted to only 7.67 per cent of the total volume. A further breakdown reveals the incredibly low figure of 0.5 per cent as Goa's trade exported to Portugal and less than 10 per cent was imported from the mother country. Goa imported Portuguese wine, sardines and olive oil at a sacrifice of eighty per cent of its share of customs duties. The adverse balance of trade increased from Rs 2.44 crores (a crore is ten million rupees) in 1946 to Rs 6.30 crores in 1951, necessitating significant subsidies from Portugal. Even Dr Oliveira Salazar, the Portuguese prime minister admitted 'financially Goa has always been a burden on the metropolitan treasury and almost from the beginning was considered by many to be ruinous for Portugal' (Salazar 1956: 425). Goa continued to be a drain on Lisbon's treasury even though in later years iron and manganese mines, developed with foreign capital, produced significant financial reserves. However, security considerations impeded the development of the economy. The railway built between 1881–87 to connect the port of Mormugao in Goa with the junction of Londa in British India was constructed on a narrow gauge to differentiate it from the rest of the subcontinent. Portuguese incentives to develop the colony declined in the 1950s because of the fear of an Indian invasion, leaving the transportation system primitive, as needed roads and bridges remained unconstructed.

While Portugal was unwilling, or unable, to afford to develop Goa economically, it attempted to stifle the colony's natural economic links with British India by imposing tariffs upon much needed rice shipments in 1938. Retaliatory customs duties on products from Goa by the British damaged indigenous agricultural industries such as coconut plantations. These measures caused a steady fall in trade between the two territories from the high figure of seventy-two per cent of all of Goa's imports coming from British India, in 1929. After independence the Indian Union accounted for about twenty per cent of Goa's imports and over forty per cent of its exports (Gaitonde and Mani 1956: 17). From its neighbour Goa imported foodgrains, fruit, vegetables, soap, coal, textiles, cotton thread, tea and tobacco. Goa's exports to India were mainly in the form of fresh fish, betel nuts, salt, and coconuts. The economic dependence of Goa on India was evidenced by the fact that Indian currency constituted almost two-thirds of all moneys in circulation in the Portuguese colony. As a result of an attempt by Portuguese authorities to ban the circulation of Indian currency from 1942 to 1952, Goans were obliged to resort to barter transactions, live on starvation rations or emigrate (P.K. Rao 1963: 58). As a result of such counter-productive economic policies, 'half the population of Goa managed to live on starvation rations, while the rest emigrated' (Kosambi 1962: 155). Aside from facilities provided for the training of priests, the only post-secondary educational institution made available by the Portuguese was the Goa Medical College. The educational backwardness of the colonies is affirmed by the fact that in 1950, 499, 455, or 78.3 per cent of the people were illiterate (United Nations 1960: 455).[7]

To secure employment and educational opportunities denied them at home, Goans—particularly males from the densely populated Old Conquests—left the colony (see Mascarenhas-Keyes 1989). It is estimated that by 1954 there were 1,800,000 Goans outside of Goa and in India, and East Africa—three times as many as remained in the colony (D'Souza 1975: 203). As many as a million Goans were residing in India—100,000 in the Bombay area alone. The fact that many were noted musicians and cooks—low caste occupations—led them to be characterized by the pejorative term 'Goanese' within British India. A great many Goans served as civil servants in Portuguese or British colonial empires in East Africa. Their emigration stabilized the population, while their remittances served to improve conditions at home (Pinto 1962). The Indian government claimed that in 1951 remittances from India to Goa totalled sixty-eight million rupees, while those from Goa to India were forty-six million rupees. By comparison, remittances from Portugal to Goa totalled only 4.1 million rupees, and remittances from Goa to Portugal amounted to 11.5 million rupees (Information Service of India n.d.: 14).

Another device employed by Goans to make up for their shortage of currency was smuggling. Expensive luxury items, far in excess of local requirements, were imported from abroad and systematically shipped illegally across the border into India without payment of customs duties. Silks, fountain pens, liquor, silver, gold and precious stones were among the commodities smuggled. The total value of contraband goods seized by Indian customs and excise authorities in three months in 1954 amounted to Rs twenty-five lakhs (a lakh is 100,000 rupees). While this figure is high, the customs department believed it had detected only about ten per cent of the total amount of goods smuggled into India (P.K. Rao 1963: 59).

However, in later years mining introduced a new dimension into the Goan economy and provided Portugal with an important source of foreign exchange. With the aid of foreign capital and Indian industrialists, mechanization was introduced after 1947 in the previously underdeveloped iron and manganese mines. Japan imported forty per cent of the 4.7 million tons of iron ore produced in 1960. Most of the remaining, thirty per cent, was shipped to West Germany. The most important customer for manganese was the United States. As Goa had two harbours, including Mormugao, one of the best in India, ore could be easily exported without Indian interference. As a result of this new found prosperity that was tied to the world economy, Goa took on the appearance of a boom town in the late 1950s.

Political Ties to India

While they were tied to the subcontinent in many respects, the Goans remained isolated from political developments in colonial India. Not until 1928 was the Goa National Congress (GNC) organized to carry the movement for independence from the British into the Portuguese possessions. This was the case even though Goan activists, many of whom were educated or employed in the Indian cities of Bombay, Poona, or Benaras, associated themselves with the Indian National Congress (INC) in its struggle to rid the subcontinent of foreign rule.

Among the leaders of the independence movement there was little doubt that the Portuguese territories were as much a part of the Indian Union as the British controlled areas. That differences in colonial rulers did not alter the fact that both Goa and the rest of the subcontinent had originally been Indian was stated by Mahatma Gandhi when he wrote in *Harijan* of September 8, 1946:

> It is ridiculous to write to Portugal [*sic*] as the motherland of Indians of Goa. Their mother country is as much India as mine. Goa is outside British India but it is within geographical India as a whole. And there is very little, if anything, in common between the Portuguese and the Indians of Goa (quoted in Bains 1962: 203).

As Prime Minister Nehru (1958b: 372) had often noted, 'The movement for freedom in India was not confined to any part of the country; its objective was freedom . . . from every kind of foreign domination.' In his opinion, the interests of the people living in Goa were 'similar or even identical' to those living in India (J. Nehru 1956: 12). The fact that Portugal occupied Goa for 450 years did not legitimate Lisbon's claim to the enclave. It only made the urgency of its union with India that much greater.

India did not feel bound by agreements made by the British and the Portuguese before it attained its own freedom. Whatever justification such islands of foreign authority had before India attained independence had disappeared on August 15, 1947. Indeed, even before independence from Britain, the Congress party in its working committee resolution at Wardha in August 1946 drew attention to the conditions in Goa when it declared:

> Goa has always been and must inevitably continue to be a part of India. It must share in the freedom of the Indian people. What its future position and status will be in a free India can only be determined in consultation with the people of Goa and not by any external authority (Rajkumar 1957: 92).

After independence was achieved, the Congress in a resolution at Jaipur in 1948 reiterated this position when it said:

With the establishment of independence in India, the continued
existence of any foreign possession in India becomes anomalous
and opposed to the conception of India's unity and freedom.
Therefore it has become necessary for these possessions to be
politically incorporated in India and no other solution can be
stable or lasting or in conformity with the will of the people
(ibid.: 97).

This position was reaffirmed two years later at Nasik and in 1952 at
Calcutta (ibid.: 105). It was to be repeated regularly, but always
without results.

However, beyond passing resolutions, the nationalist movement
virtually ignored the problem of incorporating the Portuguese
colonies during the initial years of India's independence. At the
time New Delhi secured its freedom from Great Britain, India was
preoccupied with communal strife and war with Pakistan over
Kashmir. These events served to distract the attention of the
Nehru government from the Portuguese and French pockets. After
the British left the subcontinent, New Delhi turned its attention to
convincing the French to depart from Pondicherry, which they did
in 1956.

In response to the lack of interest shown in their cause by the
Indian National Congress, the Goan revolutionaries turned to
prominent Indian socialists for support against Lisbon. Most notable
among these efforts was a demonstration organized by Socialist
Party leader Dr Ram Manohar Lohia in the south Goan city of
Margao on June 18, 1946, and *satyagraha* campaigns led by Praja
Socialist Party leaders in 1954 and 1955.[8] Despite the fact that the
Portuguese response to these tactics was repressive, the Nehru
government refused to intervene. In fact, Indian interest in Goa
seemed to wane despite official Congress resolutions. T.B. Cunha,
the most prominent Goan revolutionary, commented on this un-
expected lack of support:

> . . . at one time the Indian National Congress, the main organ-
> ization working for our freedom, had recognized the Goa Con-
> gress Committee by giving us a representation in the All-India
> Congress Committee. But that lasted only a few years, and
> suddenly our committee was considered foreign and disaffiliated
> (Cunha 1961: 195).

Cunha (1958: 473) blamed Indian business for sabotaging Congress efforts to free Goa. According to him, businessmen who operated in India as well as Goa were given preferential treatment by Portuguese authorities desirous of building up the colony's economy. He further maintained that Nehru's caution resulted from pressure that the Vatican exerted on behalf of Portugal (Cunha 1957: 7, 14).

Status of Goans in India before 1961

Their existing political differences and cultural similarities made the status of Goans in India ambiguous. Hence they were treated as citizens by India as well as by Portugal. Accordingly, the claim could be made in the House of the People that, 'Goans are treated as *de facto* Indians for all practical purposes and do not suffer from any special disability.'[9] According to Deputy Minister of External Affairs, Lakshmi Menon, 'All Goans who had their domicile in India and had been ordinarily resident in India for not less than five years immediately before 26 January 1950 are eligible, if they are otherwise qualified for registration, as voters.'[10]

Even though Goans were permitted most of the same rights enjoyed by Indians before their incorporation in December 1961, Prime Minister Nehru was cognizant of the reality that many appreciated the differences that had arisen in 450 years of Portuguese occupation. He, therefore, made certain commitments about Goa's future status after incorporation that would protect its autonomy. These assurances were:

(*a*) The freedom and rights guaranteed by the Constitution of India and which specifically refer to freedom of conscience, worship and practice of religions, will extend in full measure and in all their implications to these areas.

(*b*) The special circumstances of cultural, social and lingual relations and the sense of territorial group which history has created will be respected.

(*c*) Laws and customs which are part of the social pattern of these areas and which are consistent with fundamental human rights and freedoms, will be respected and modifications will be sought only by negotiation and consent.

(*d*) As we have done in the rest of India, full use will be made
of the administrative, judicial and other services, confident
that the return of freedom to and the unity of these areas
with the motherland will enable adjustments to be made in
harmony with progress and with the desires of the people
(J. Nehru 1958b: 375).

In addition to these guarantees, India pledged to preserve the
tomb of St Francis Xavier, a sacred Roman Catholic shrine. The
Portuguese conceded that, 'We have no doubt that India would
give us not only such an assurance, but also many other guarantees
which we might seek in various fields . . . .'[11] However, Lisbon
was adamant that it could not negotiate sovereignty over territory
it viewed as an integral part of its country—a claim that not even
Britain had dared make. This intransigent position served only to
infuriate Prime Minister Nehru, who said that Portugal had entertained a proposal from the Nizam of Hyderabad to transfer Goa to
it when the princely state was resisting integration with India in
1948.[12]

The Portuguese colonies on the Indian Subcontinent lasted longer
than did those of the French, but the influence of Lisbon was not
as enduring as was that of Paris. The violent nature of their
departure ensured that the Portuguese, unlike the French who left
Pondicherry voluntarily, had little say in preserving their culture in
Goa.

END NOTES

1. The most noted historical works describing Portuguese colonization and policy
   on the subcontinent are Boxer (1969), Danvers (1894) and Whiteway (1899).
2. For excellent description of Goa under the Portuguese see Kosambi (1962:
   chapter 5) and Historical Society of the Foreign Office (1920).
3. For this line of thought see Pattee (1957), [Remy] (1957) and Saldanna (1957).
4. 'Political and Economic Conditions in Goa,' March 5, 1947, pp 1–4, State
   Department Central Files, 853.00/3–547.
5. *New York Times,* December 12, 1952, p. 6.
6. India, *Lok Sabha Debates,* Third Series, Vol.III, No. 26, May 21, 1962,
   columns 5539–40.
7. The corresponding illiteracy rate for the Indian Union at the time was 83.4 per
   cent (United Nations 1960: 443).
8. One source (Bhargava 1955: 6–9), maintains that Nehru refused to assist the
   campaign because he was not anxious to support a socialist cause. Lohia,

himself, wrote, 'The Portuguese took their measure of India's rulers . . . .
They saw clearly that these rulers were false and small men . . . whose words
made a lot of noise but whose acts rarely kept step with them.' Foreword to
Kulkarni (1956: iii). Lohia was particularly critical of the Congress leadership
in the Bombay area for its lack of support.

9. India, *Lok Sabha Debates*, Second Series, Vol. LIV, No. 44, April 14, 1961,
column 11321.
10. Ibid., Vol. LVII, No. 16, August 28, 1961, column 5119.
11. *New York Times*, August 18, 1954, p. 28.
12. *Hindustan Overseas Times* (New Delhi), September 2, 1954 and Gopal (1979:
41).

Chapter 3

Territorial Integration

◆

The territorial integration of Goa into the Indian Union reaffirms Walker Connor's thesis that international frontiers are usually redrawn by armed force not by argument or majority votes (Connor 1994: 23). This chapter reviews India's fourteen years of diplomatic effort to persuade Portugal, as did France, to vacate its colonial possessions on the subcontinent. It also discusses the unsuccessful efforts of domestic political activists to expel the Portuguese through non-violent *satyagraha* campaigns. Since the myriad of splinter groups that claimed to be working to liberate Goa were unable to coordinate their activities (see Esteves 1986: 55), it determines that international pressure finally led India to abandon its commitment to the peaceful resolution of international disputes. When Prime Minister Nehru finally decided to employ armed force to eject the Portuguese in December 1961, it was primarily in response to African rather than either Goan or domestic political influence (see A. Rubinoff 1971; Deora 1995; Shadi 1962: 129).[1]

The Symbolic Nature of the Dispute

Without question, Goa had a symbolic importance for both the Portuguese and the Indians. The Portuguese, having been the first European power to arrive in Asia and the last to depart, regarded continued possession of territory on the Indian subcontinent as a symbol of their prestige. For the Indians, foreign occupation of Goa was not only a stain upon their honour, but also a reminder of an unhappy colonial past that was not completely ended. Portugal's presence on Indian soil also undermined New Delhi's claim to leadership of the Afro-Asian movement. Prime Minister Nehru stated the problem in a speech in Uttar Pradesh on August 21, 1955:

> Opposed as we are to colonialism everywhere, it is impossible for us to tolerate the continuation of colonial rule in a small part of India. It is not that we covet Goa. That little bit of territory makes no difference to this great country. But even a small enclave under foreign rule does make a difference, and it is a constant reproach to the self-respect and national interest of India (Quoted by Palmer 1958: 294).

So far as the Portuguese were concerned, the status of Goa became a matter of dispute 'the moment the Indian Union became independent' (Salazar 1962: 12). India refused to be bound by agreements made by the British before 1947. As the prime minister told the Parliament on October 1, 1951, 'Whatever justification such islands of foreign authority had when India was a subject country disappeared with the coming of independence to India.'[2]

India's blunder, as Joachim Alva, a member of Parliament of Goan descent, was later to say, 'was that in 1947 it did not occupy Goa without any notice and without ultimatum.'[3] Since neither France nor Portugal could possibly have maintained their enclaves in India without British support, India should have attempted to press for a general agreement that would have brought independence to all foreign possessions at the same time. But according to Prime Minister Nehru (1956: 8–9), Indians

> did not trouble [them]selves about them because [they] felt that the moment the British power in India was removed, automatically, inevitably, these other parts and enclaves, whether under the French or the Portuguese would naturally revert to the motherland. There was no doubt about it. I must confess that it never occurred to me for a minute in those old days that we would have any controversy with the French Government or the Portuguese Government over these possessions. So far as the Portuguese were concerned, we were not acquainted with their Government . . . .

It is also true, however, that Prime Minister Jawaharlal Nehru, who took office in 1946, had been preoccupied with the partition of the country with Pakistan and related issues like the Kashmir dispute. In any event, the most logical opportunity for an amicable settlement of the Portuguese possessions—the transfer of British power on the Indian subcontinent—was missed.

In the words of one commentator, the problem of Goa had become 'a problem of two prestige-ridden Prime Ministers; and so long as it remains on this footing, it will not have a solution' ([Goman-taki] 1957: 206). Prime Minister Salazar (1956: 431) issued Nehru a direct challenge to live up to his commitment to peaceful methods. The Portuguese leader envisaged three possible solutions to the Goa problem: one was by violent means and the remainder entailed pacific methods. The first choice the Portuguese dictator offered India was the use of force to obtain the integration of the Portuguese possessions on the subcontinent. Dr Salazar acknowledged Indian military superiority when he wrote, 'It cannot be doubted she [India] has the means to take possession against such resistance as the Portuguese forces there might be able to offer.' However, since the Portuguese felt a 'moral duty' to resist, this would serve to make Nehru's victory embarrassing.

Nor was it possible for India to follow the second option and ignore Goa. Goa had too many affinities and interlocking commercial interests with India for this alternative to be practical. As this policy would prohibit mass meetings, marches, and propaganda from originating on the Indian side of the border, the people of Goa would be constrained by such a course. So far as Dr Salazar was concerned, the 'only genuine solution' of the problem was for India to practice its professed doctrine of peaceful coexistence. Yet this alternative denied India its goal of incorporating Goa.

The dilemma for Nehru was obvious. He was the head of government of a democratic country that had gained independence by non-violent means. His antagonist was a fascist dictatorship that had gained power by violent revolution and was now championing peaceful methods. In order to be faithful to the Gandhian emphasis on means he would have to leave his own colonial revolution uncompleted. Although a leader of the anti-colonial states and believing in the justice of their cause, he was also committed morally and intellectually to the pacific settlement of disputes. Any diplomatic problem that put these roles in conflict was certain to be a continuing challenge as well as a provocation. For fourteen years Goa presented itself as such an issue; for the Portuguese presence, while rendering proof of Nehru's western admired commitment to non-violence, eroded his revolutionary image in most of the world. Yet any attempt to remove the reluctant colonial power would render the Indian prime minister vulnerable to the charge of hypocrisy. It was a situation the Portuguese could not help exploiting.

To the disdain of most of his countrymen, Prime Minister Nehru followed the third and then the second of Portugal's alternatives before resorting in the end to the first. Nehru pursued peaceful methods for fourteen years because he believed that the restraint he showed over Goa would not alienate Portugal's NATO allies. He deemed this factor to be more important than the approval a display of force would bring from the communist and neutral countries. In this way the Indian leader believed he was helping to mitigate the tensions of the cold war. As a man of peace, he was sincerely interested in preserving India's non-violent image in world politics. He believed that 'inevitably'[4] Goa would be integrated into the Indian Union. In the meantime he told the Parliament that India would profit from her nuisances, for 'Possibly when history comes to be written, Kashmir and Goa will be the brightest examples of our tolerance, of our patience, and the way we have even suppressed our anger and resentment at many things, in order to follow the broad idealistic policy that we have laid down.'[5]

The Policy of Negotiations

The French Departure

After securing independence from Britain, Prime Minister Nehru decided to put no real pressure on the Portuguese to abandon their territories in India until he had persuaded the French to withdraw from the subcontinent. Hoping that Lisbon would follow the French example, Nehru first concentrated on bringing the five French settlements into the Indian Union. As the populace of these areas had been agitating for merger, France began facing the inevitable as early as 1947. At that time Paris began discussions with New

Delhi on a possible solution that preserved the cultural identity of the French possessions after they became part of India (see Miles 1995; Parker 1955; Poplai 1959; Rajkumar 1951; Lok Sabha Secretariat 1966: 207–16). Despite some initial hesitation, the government of Pierre Mendes-France, after withdrawing from Indo-China, agreed to leave India. In October 1954 the French settlements were transferred *de facto* to India. By 1956 an agreement was signed giving India complete control over the areas ('Treaty of Succession of the French Establishments of Pondicherry, Karaikal, Mahe, and Yanam', 1956). The treaty reached over Pondicherry justified Nehru's reliance on peaceful methods. He stated, 'That is what I call a real solution, and if you proceed along with right methods, they may be tedious and slow at times, but ultimately in order to solve a problem fully and completely that path is the quickest' (J. Nehru 1956: 20).

However, Nehru soon realized that the French and Portuguese situations were not the same. For one thing it was easier for France to leave the subcontinent after surrendering more significant territories in Indo-China; the Portuguese regarded their Indian possessions as more important to their Empire than did the French. For another, the inhabitants of the Portuguese enclaves were not demanding integration into the Indian Union. They seemed at best to be apathetic.

Diplomatic Efforts

For these reasons the Indian government did not pay much attention to the Goa problem in its early years. Whatever interest was expressed came from private groups in India. Finally four years after independence from the British, Prime Minister Nehru rose in Parliament on March 28, 1951, and made clear his policy regarding foreign possessions. While refusing to issue an ultimatum, he said:

India cannot tolerate any footholds of foreign powers in this country. We are anxious to give people in these areas the opportunity to live their own life and the right to change their future. We do not wish to interfere with their ways of life. There are only two ways of bringing this about—either through war or through diplomatic means. In pursuance of ideals, we have ruled out war as a means of redress, unless we are forced into one. The only alternative we are left with is the diplomatic one and we are pursuing it (J. Nehru 1958a: 194).

In pursuit of these diplomatic methods, India had opened a legation in Lisbon in 1949 for the expressed purpose of establishing contacts for a negotiated settlement (B.K. Nehru 1962: 5). Nehru's critics accused the prime minister of failing to assert Indian sovereignty over Goa and surrendering rights which India had already possessed. Nevertheless, on February 27, 1950, India approached Portugal with a request to begin talks on the disposition of its territories on the Indian subcontinent. On August 14 of that same year, Nehru announced that the Portuguese had rejected the initiative.[6] By January 1953 India submitted a further note suggesting that Portugal transfer the enclaves to India and later make a shift of administration. When Lisbon declared it could not discuss the question, let alone accept the solution offered by India, the Nehru government, claiming it had ceased to be of practical utility, closed India's legation in Lisbon on June 11, 1953.[7] Salazar responded by stating that Portugal would retain a legation in New Delhi in order to promote good relations between the two countries.[8]

India had earlier ordered a Portuguese bank in Bombay closed in retaliation against 'discriminatory' treatment accorded to Indian banks that operated in Goa. Relations between the two countries continued to deteriorate when in March 1954 the Nehru government announced severe restrictions on the free movement of Goan officials within India. The action was said to be in retaliation against similar treatment accorded to Indian visitors to Goa. Just as Indians had to register within seventy-two hours and report regularly to the police in Goa, officials from the Portuguese colony visiting India now had to obtain permits and identification from the Indian consul-general in Goa.[9]

Satyagraha Campaigns

With the failure of the diplomatic efforts, a Goa National Committee was established in 1953 to coordinate activities of all the diverse Goan nationalist parties. This development initiated a period of greater intensification of the campaign to bring Goa into the Indian Union. Plans were organized in 1954 for *satyagraha* (non-violent defiance of illegitimate authority) demonstrations by prominent Goan citizens. One leader, a noted surgeon Dr P.S. Gaitonde, was jailed and later exiled for refusing to toast the Portuguese government (see Gaitonde 1987). Nationalist demonstrations in which the Indian flag was raised were held on June 18, the anniversary of the 1946 uprising. Over twenty participants were arrested by the local authorities. New Delhi sent a strong note of protest, holding the Portuguese responsible for the consequences of whatever followed. The note warned, 'The Indian Government could not continue to remain a silent spectator of the continuance of the repressive policy hereto followed by the Portuguese authorities.'[10]

The Integration of Dadra and Nagar Haveli

On July 22 about thirty-five volunteers occupied the enclave of Dadra, south of Daman, and hoisted the Indian flag. Two defenders were killed and five others were wounded during the skirmish.[11] Although the liberators had requested merger with India, the Nehru government maintained it had no knowledge of the invasion until after the events.[12] Shortly thereafter the nearby enclave of Nagar Haveli was occupied by two groups of volunteers, one from the 'Free Goa' movement backed by the nationalist–communal-oriented Jana Sangh and the other from the left-wing Goan Peoples' Party. The Portuguese defenders resisted for several days and requested permission from the Nehru government to move troops across Indian territory to reinforce the enclaves. In a vigorous refusal the Indian government stated, 'We do not and cannot permit the movement of foreign troops or police on Indian soil and certainly cannot be a party to the suppression of a genuine nationalist movement for freedom from foreign rule.'[13]

These incidents led to another round of expulsions of diplomatic personnel. The Portuguese gave the Indian consul-general in Goa and the vice consul at Mormugao until July 31, or twenty-four hours, to leave. In reprisal, India immediately ordered the Portuguese consul-general in Bombay to depart within forty-eight hours, or by August 1.[14] Consular relations were not re-established until January 18, 1955.

The 1954 Failure

In the meantime affiliates of India's Praja Socialist Party, without notifying either the Congress party or the government, announced plans for a *satyagraha* march into Goa. The demonstration was scheduled for August 15, the day of Indian independence. Four to six thousand persons were expected to participate. The Portuguese immediately reinforced Goa, Daman and Diu, and on August 7 placed the colonies on a war footing. Its soldiers given 'shoot to kill orders,' Portugal took a number of concurrent actions: rail and ferry services were suspended; highways and bridges were mined; trenches were dug; all foreign newspapers and journals were banned; schools were closed; and a night curfew was established.[15] Although accused of mass troop build up on the border, the most the Indian government appears to have contributed to the tensions was additional economic sanctions. New Delhi prohibited transfer of Indian currency through the mail to Goa which was very dependent on remittances. Sums of cash allowed to visitors were also further reduced.[16] As these sanctions caused resentment among hard-pressed Goans, they were relaxed within a few days.[17]

Instead of supporting the proposed march, the Indian government discouraged it. As his biographer Frank Moraes (1956: 291–92) noted, for most of his life Prime Minister Nehru had resisted the idea that non-violence should be projected to the sphere of defence against external aggression.[18] Hence, he declared that the marchers, who had to pledge to be non-violent, had to be composed entirely of Goans—not Indians. To reinforce these stipulations, Indian police prevented their nationals from crossing the frontier and searched those Goans permitted across the border for arms.[19]

As a consequence of these constraints, the marchers dwindled to a pathetic forty-seven participants, most of them teenagers. All of the demonstrators were immediately arrested by Portuguese authorities. Since Prime Minister Nehru (1958b: 372) had proclaimed, 'This is an entirely Goan movement, popular and indigenous,' Portuguese Foreign Minister Paulo Cunha ridiculed India by expressing the belief that the recent farce showed no Goans cared to revolt.[20]

Prime Minister Nehru (1958b: 373) defended his decisions before the Lok Sabha on August 25. He claimed his policies would not abandon 'the cause of our compatriots under Portuguese rule' or deliberately provoke violence.

Notwithstanding this benevolent policy, Portugal was winning the battle of public relations. On August 8 it proposed that an international commission be established to permit neutral observers to inspect Goa's border. While India readily agreed to this measure, it refused to accede to the Portuguese demand that observers be sent to the occupied territories of Dadra and Nagar Haveli. Joint talks to implement the process broke down when India wanted to discuss the transfer of the enclaves, something Lisbon found unacceptable.

The 1955 Bloodshed

Despite these efforts at accommodation, the tension between India and Portugal did not diminish. Portugal threatened to fight intruders with all the means at its disposal and asserted that New Delhi had no right to pass judgement on the severity of penalties imposed upon those arrested in Goa, even if some of those exiled to Lisbon were Indian nationals. These arrests and reports of ill-treatment of *satyagrahis* (activists following the path of non-violence or *Satyagraha*) led to increased strain in May 1955, when Indian volunteers began crossing the border without interference from their government. When the Government of India failed to demonstrate active support for the demonstrators, the Praja Socialist, Mazdoor Kisan, Hindu Mahasabha and Communist parties announced plans to organize the marchers. An All-Party Parliamentary Committee for Goa with the aim of mobilizing Indian public opinion, was formed on May 5. In response to their drive, thousands of *satyagrahis*, including several members of Parliament, entered Goa in small groups.[21] Although few were injured, and all the leaders were released, the demonstrators had succeeded in embarrassing the Congress party and the Government of India. With the opposition demanding a police action or at least a peaceful invasion, the ruling party appeared to have lost the initiative in Indian politics for the first time.

Despite sentiment for a more militant course in the Congress executive, Nehru firmly refused to officially sanction the *satyagraha* campaign. At a two-hour press conference in Delhi on May 31, the longest on record up to that time, the prime minister reiterated his hope that Goans, not Indians, would spearhead the movement for their own liberation.[22] As far as he was concerned, individual Indians could march into Goa—but not in large numbers.

It was his view that a mass civilian invasion as contemplated by the opposition could only lead to violence.

It was Nehru's expressed belief that *satyagraha* was a technique which could be correctly employed by the people to bring pressure only on their own government. Hence, he announced that any demonstrations by Indians in Goa would be regarded as directed against his own administration not the Portuguese.[23] *Satyagraha*, he held, could not be performed by one government against another. To do so, he told the Lok Sabha on July 26, would be a misapplication of the method (J. Nehru 1958b: 383–84).

However, as the summer wore on the prime minister seemed to modify his position. Even if he had not pledged government support, he assured congressmen who desired to participate in the proposed Independence Day *satyagraha*, he would not interfere as he had done a year earlier. When the Praja Socialist Party took the lead in organizing marches into Goa, Nehru had been quoted as saying, 'I admire the courage of those who want to go there.'[24] There were other indications of tacit support by the ambivalent prime minister. At the very time when he was urging restraint in Parliament, additional sanctions were being applied by the Government of India against Goa. It was announced that all rail traffic was being suspended because of 'something in the nature of mines planted under the tracks.'[25] Nehru further ordered the Portuguese to close their legation in Delhi by August 8. He claimed he was taking this 'drastic action' to prove the Congress party was as opposed to Portuguese rule in Goa as any other group in India.[26] Yet, he refrained from completely breaking-off relations between the two governments.

Nehru's half-measures did not satisfy his critics. Dissatisfied dock workers in Bombay, Calcutta and Madras decided not to work on any ship that had carried cargo bound for Goa or picked up goods in that port. They also threatened not to handle any ship of a line that had other vessels docked there. By now there was no Indian sea, air or rail traffic to the Portuguese colonies and they had become some of the 'least accessible places in Asia.'[27] Moreover, the only auto route that ran 120 miles through jungle and mountains from Belgaum was closed to all traffic except correspondents. In support of the approaching demonstrations an effective sympathy strike was staged by 150,000 textile, railway and dock workers throughout India.

On the appointed day of August 15 several thousand marchers entered Goa, Daman and Diu. Although the Portuguese withdrew from their immediate border positions, approximately twenty demonstrators were killed and over two hundred injured. As the *Economist* wrote, deaths are not a surprising outcome when a few isolated police men are approached by a mob of 2000 demonstrators, even if it is unarmed.[28]

The next day in Parliament, Prime Minister Nehru denounced the Portuguese behaviour as brutal and uncivilized, while both Houses adjourned for a half hour in memory of those killed. The Indian people, however, responded in a less restrained fashion. *Hartals*, or sympathy riots, and protest strikes took place in several major cities. In Bombay, crowds attacked the Portuguese consulate and offices of the British deputy commissioner and the Pakistani assistant high commissioner. In Calcutta, a day of mourning was declared as the Portuguese consulate was stormed by students who hoisted the Indian flag. Violent strikes also took place in Delhi. More deaths and injuries resulted from these incidents than could be attributed to the Portuguese firings. As a result of these criminal activities, a potential propaganda coup was turned into a public relations debacle.

While the Nehru government was assailed by segments of western press for the assault on diplomatic institutions, it was also under attack at home for its refusal to give official backing to the *satya-grahis*. Accusing the Indian government for being responsible for the death of civilians, the communist organ *New Age* claimed:

> As the ruling party and a leading party in the country, the people expected the Congress to give the lead in taking effective steps to liberate Goa. But the Congress maintained that it was for the Goans to fight for liberation though, no doubt, such an approach falsified the understanding that Goans were Indians and Goa was a part of India. When Kashmir was attacked it was not left to the Kashmiris to defend themselves.[29]

The prime minister did not use an outraged citizenry as an excuse to invade Goa in retaliation for the Portuguese shootings. He responded to the Portuguese firings with characteristic half-measures. India completely broke off diplomatic ties with Portugal as an expression of condemnation for the August 15, 1955 killings.

Lisbon was given until September 1 to close its consulate in Bombay and honorary consulates in Madras and Calcutta. At the same time India withdrew its last official listening post in Goa by closing its consulate-general in Panjim.[30] Defying public opinion and segments of his own party, Nehru declared that his government did not intend to have its policies 'directed from the marketplace'.[31] Even though he was by now 'almost single-handedly' resisting the demand for invasion (B.K. Nehru 1962: 7), Prime Minister Nehru proved his control over the Congress party and hence the government by convincing them with an implied threat of resignation to forbid any demonstrators—even non-violent ones—from entering the Portuguese territories (see Chary 1955). As the Goa question was revived every August,[32] Prime Minister Nehru had to make it appear that his commitment to liberate Goa was not lessening. He thus felt compelled to take additional measures against Portugal from time-to-time, but these sanctions only served to alienate lower-class Goans. Moreover, Goa's changing economy made the Portuguese less dependent on India's transportation system.

The Return to Diplomatic Methods

After the ill-fated 1954–55 *satyagraha* campaigns, the Nehru government returned to its earlier policy of attempting to peacefully settle the question of the disposition of the Portuguese territories in India. Nehru was convinced 'a wrong direction has been given to the movement for the liberation of Goa.' Accordingly, he wrote to the country's chief ministers, 'It does not matter much if the solution of the problem is delayed by a year or two' (Parthasarathi 1988: 261). Speaking before the Lok Sabha on September 17, the prime minister declared:

> There is nothing I can argue with any person who thinks that the methods employed in regard to Goa must be other than peaceful, because we rule out non-peaceful methods completely . . . . One cannot have it both ways. Either one adopts military methods or police action or one keeps to peaceful methods. To mix them up is to fall between two policies, and to be nowhere . . . . If we suddenly reverse our policy, the world will get an opportunity to say that we are deceitful . . . . Once we accept the position that

we can use the Army for the solution of our problems, we cannot deny the same right to other countries. It is a question of principle (J. Nehru 1958b: 386–91).

The prime minister urged the members of Parliament not to just take a nationalistic view, but also consider the international consequences of their actions in Goa. He then invited the Portuguese to do the same and transfer their colonies on the subcontinent to India. Nehru reminded Lisbon that although pledged to non-violence, India, like any other country had military and police forces. Yet, at the same time, he reiterated his pledge to not provoke a war and use force only in defence.

That Nehru was able to maintain this position for six years was a tribute to his statesmanship. If an invasion was not forthcoming, a political debate was now underway. The opposition, especially the Hindu communal parties, attacked the government in the public arena for undercutting Goa's freedom movement. As it became apparent that the Goans themselves were not responding to their efforts, the parties of the right and left pursued a more moderate course. For six years they restricted their activities to holding meetings, passing resolutions, and publicizing atrocities the Portuguese allegedly committed in Goa. Ironically, the Communist Party, often anxious to exploit situations of violence in Indian politics, was in the late 1950s anxious to prove it could act as a responsible opposition and did its utmost to avoid being identified with campaigns of direct action (Overstreet and Windmiller 1959: 323). By April 1958 the Goa National Congress, organizer of the 1955 demonstrations, ended its active role and urged the government to seek a peaceful solution. As Mr Nehru refused to permit political demonstrators from India to enter the Portuguese territories, 'consciously or unconsciously, the government assumed responsibility for freeing those areas' (P.K. Rao 1963: 131).

The Policy of Liberalization

With the relaxation of domestic pressure, the Indian government embarked on a campaign to win the support of the Goan people. Travel restrictions were abolished,[33] and telegraph services which had been cut in September 1955 were restored.[34] On February 28, 1961 the Ministry of External Affairs told Parliament that as of

April 1 the government was resuming limited trade with Goa.[35] Prime Minister Nehru explained that his 'policy of liberalization'[36] was designed to assist the poorer classes in the Portuguese colonies. Later that autumn he announced that money order remittances to Goa had resumed on the fifteenth of October.[37]

The International Dimension

Following the unsuccessful *satyagraha* campaign, the Government of India embarked on a drive to educate its people and world opinion on the merits of its position and the evils of Portuguese colonialism. Portugal's policy during the ensuing period was to forestall any provocation that would give Prime Minister Nehru the pretext for a police action, and thus, instead of India, emerge as the champion of peaceful coexistence. Goa, as the symbol of colonialism, became the acid test in judging India's relations with other countries (Streiff 1955: 4). If there was a tendency in India to exaggerate the importance of this question, there was likewise a disturbing inclination in the West to minimize or even ignore the issue because it was regarded as having little or no rational justification. In fact the Goa situation was doubly sensitive because it juxtaposed the twin Indian evils of colonialism and alliances. As Portugal was aligned with the United States and Great Britain, it attempted to make Goa a cold war issue. Their identification with colonialism and alliances put the western countries at a considerable disadvantage with the Soviets in the competition for the allegiance of India and other developing states. By urging the United States and Great Britain to take the lead in settling the dispute, Prime Minister Nehru attempted to prevent Goa from becoming involved in the struggle between the rival blocs. Although India appeared to be drawing closer to Great Britain and the United States, neither country acted on India's invitations to mediate the Goa controversy.[38] Caught between feelings of enlightened colonial policy and alliance commitments, neither country could afford to take sides. Nor did they use influence with their ally Portugal to resolve the dispute peacefully. As long as Lisbon was reminding the world of Portugal's alliance partners, it was impossible for London and Washington to appear neutral about Goa.

Great Britain

The British were caught between supporting a former colony and Commonwealth partner, India, and 'an ally of such long standing as Portugal.'[39] The Anglo-Portuguese alliance dates from 1373. Dr Salazar made it clear that he believed that Portugal's sovereignty over its Indian possessions was guaranteed by the Anglo-Portuguese Treaty of 1642.[40] The most important bilateral treaty affecting the Goa problem, however, was the agreement signed between England and Portugal in 1661. England had promised to defend and protect all conquests or colonies belonging to Portugal from future as well as present enemies (for the text of these agreements see Rao 1956: 61–67). However, this provision applied to only external attack and not to civil wars or internal uprisings. These commitments were reaffirmed as late as 1899, and during World War II Britain had invoked them to obtain base facilities in the Azores. Thus theoretically at any rate, Great Britain was pledged to defend Goa against Indian attack but not against a Goan revolt.[41] Moreover, the Portuguese case with respect to the Goa issue had important support in journalistic and political circles in Great Britain (see Rajan 1960–61: 161). While the Indian reaction was totally out of proportion to Britain's commitment to Portugal, the spectre of two NATO allies strengthening historic ties in South Asia was reinforced by propaganda which emanated from the Soviet Union and the Indian Communist Party.

NATO

Article V of the North Atlantic Treaty Organization (NATO) signed on April 4, 1949 by Portugal contains a pledge by the contracting parties that 'an armed attack against one or more of them in Europe or North America shall be considered an attack against them all' (Quotations in this section are taken from NATO Information Service 1965: 210–11). Consequently, in the event of such an attack each of them was obligated to 'assist the party or parties so attacked.' Although Article VI of this agreement speci- fically limits the response of the parties to attacks in either Europe or North America, Portugal sought to invoke Article IV which provides that the other parties, 'will consult together whenever in the opinion of any of them, the territorial integrity, political independence or security of any party is threatened.' As Portugal had considered Goa to be an integral part of its territory since 1952, Lisbon had enjoyed some success in getting NATO partners to support its claim in India. However, in 1954 the North Atlantic Treaty Organization decided Portugal was entitled to ask for help, but could not expect to receive it in the case of Goa because the territory was outside the jurisdiction protected by the treaty.[42] Nevertheless, Portugal continued to submit reports on the Indian situation to the North Atlantic Treaty Organization.

The mere fact that NATO would have to at least consider assisting Portugal against India was enough to enrage Prime Minister Nehru. Seldom did he discuss the Goa issue without bringing up Portugal's connection with NATO. At the Bandung conference in 1955 Nehru castigated Portugal's alliance partners for insisting India not take action in Goa (Kahin 1956: 68–69). In his estimation, 'any alliance that has a country like Portugal as a member . . . does not raise its status in the eyes of people.'[43]

There were other reasons why the Indians felt uneasy about Portugal's membership in NATO. In the event of a war between the United States and the Soviet Union, Nehru was fearful that Portugal's base in Goa would bring the conflict to the subcontinent (J. Nehru 1956: 11). Similarly, as Portugal had ceded Timor to Japan to use against its British ally Australia in World War II, there was genuine apprehension that arch-enemy Pakistan, with its role in the South East Asian Treaty Organization and the Baghdad Pact, would someday be the recipient of Goa. For their part the Pakistanis did the utmost to encourage such a notion. Not only did they side with the Portuguese cause, but they courted Lisbon in economic matters and sent visiting diplomatic missions to Goa. The Indians viewed this behaviour as 'the most outstanding instance of Pakistan's hostility towards India in world affairs on a matter absolutely unconnected with their bilateral relations . . .' (Rajan 1967: 506). At the very least, as India's Minister of Defence Krishna Menon pointed out, Lisbon's membership in NATO permitted alliance troops to train in Portugal and freed up resources for use elsewhere in places like Goa.[44]

The United States

The Goa affair highlights American–Indian misunderstandings. Until the dispatch of the aircraft-carrier *Enterprise* to the Bay of Bengal during the 1971 Indo-Pakistan war that resulted in the creation of Bangladesh (see van Hollen 1980), no other issue symbolized the difficulties in bilateral relations more than Goa. The magnitude of antagonism voiced by both the press and officials of the American government over the issue of the Portuguese colonies on the subcontinent, and the comparable Indian reaction to it, are evidence of the degree of mutual disillusionment that characterized relations between the two countries. This disenchantment, which had long been beneath the surface, stemmed from the lack of commitment shown by the United States towards the anti-colonial struggle and the failure of India to become aligned against international communism. The differences in priorities were obvious. India, concentrating on internal development and following a policy of non-alignment, frowned on military pacts directed against ideological abstractions in times of peace. United States, on the other hand, preoccupied with what it believed to be a monolithic communist threat, failed to show interest in the peaceful resolution of a colonial problem that involved a NATO partner. However, as Prime Minister Nehru remarked, Goa was an issue that constantly agitated the Indian people since they were constantly confronted by it (Cited from a 'Meet the Press' television interview in Indian Embassy 1961: 65). By the same token, the American government did not appreciate that India might employ force against a weak country like Portugal while Prime Minister Nehru constantly urged the United States to employ restraint in its dealings with the Soviet Union.

The American connection with the colonial power that occupied Goa made the United States the target of India's Communist Party and other groups that desired to associate Washington with imperialism in South Asia. A typical communist publication asserted:

The Americans want Goa (thinly camouflaged under the Portuguese flag) for three purposes. Firstly, Goa is an important harbour in the sea-route from the Middle East to South East Asia. This is why, in recent years the U.S.A. has spent huge amounts deepening and broadening the Marmugao harbour and improving its port facilities and technical equipment. Ship loads of American arms have been coming to Goa in rapid succession. They have also constructed huge military aerodromes near the harbour.

The territory around Goa is rich in iron and manganese deposits which is the second attraction for the Americans. Thirdly, Goa is like a thorn in India's loins which can always be used by the Anglo-Americans as a potential threat to her security (Sardesai 1953: 8).

While the United States was forced to deny that all of these allegations were without foundation,[45] the fact that they were still believed by many Indians kept Washington on the defensive.

Yet, the Americans did little to correct the prevailing image. Secretary of State John Foster Dulles, in a series of provocative statements, seemed to reinforce Indian suspicions only a few months after John Sherman Cooper, the ambassador to India issued a much appreciated statement registering American opposition to colonialism.[46] Meanwhile in the United States as Dulles' guest, Portuguese Foreign Minister Paulo Cunha, charged before the National Press Club that India was guilty of imperialism.[47] A joint communiqué released on December 2, 1955 by the two diplomats referred to the 'Portuguese provinces in the Far East,'[48] and implied that Goa was an integral part of Portugal and not a colony. Despite an assurance by Ambassador Cooper that the United States had not made a decision to oppose Indian claims,[49] Dulles aggravated the damage at a press conference on December 6 when he remarked about Goa, 'As far as I know, all the world regards it as a Portuguese province.'[50] Despite the efforts of Governor Averell Harriman of New York[51] and Senator Hubert Humphrey of Minnesota[52] to downplay the significance of what he said, Dr Rajendra Prasad, India's president, in a rare public statement claimed that Dulles as an international lawyer knew exactly what he meant.[53] As Prime Minister Nehru later understated, Secretary of State Dulles' comment 'had made the solution of the Goa issue more difficult.'[54]

Dulles' remarks were particularly damaging because the Soviet Premier Nikolai Bulganin and Communist Party Secretary, Nikita Khrushchev, were touring India castigating American imperialism at the time (For their remarks see Gupta 1962: 12–13). That they took advantage of the situation is evidenced by a reporter who wrote, 'Nothing made Bulganin and Khrushchev more popular . . . than their forceful denunciation of Portuguese colonialism in Goa' (Raghaven 1956: 64). Assisted by Secretary of State Dulles,[55] they implanted in India doubts about America's professed anti-imperialism. It was this undertone of mutual resentment which was to be resurrected by the American reaction to the 1961 invasion.

The Departure from Peaceful Methods

If anything, Prime Minister Nehru's attitude towards the Portuguese seemed to be mellowing as prospects of integrating Lisbon's colonies on the subcontinent receded. For fourteen years Nehru had resisted pleas within the Congress party leadership and from both Houses of Parliament that he take more energetic action. As late as December 1960 Nehru had told Parliament that he could not fix a date when the Portuguese would be out of Goa.[56] The next March Prime Minister Nehru, in a major policy decision, decided to send 3000 troops to the Congo as part of United Nations peacekeeping forces. As the year progressed, it became increasingly more difficult to justify employment of military in Africa while there was inaction in Goa and a growing Chinese threat in the Himalayas. By the fall of 1961 neither India nor the world was certain if the Nehru government was still committed to a peaceful solution to the Goa problem. As manifestos were issued for India's third general election scheduled for January 1962—an election which Defence Minister Krishna Menon was contesting from the heavily Goan electoral district of North Bombay (see Palmer 1963: 129)—every party but the pro-western Swatantra had a Goa plank in their platforms, and all were considerably more militant than that proposed by the Congress.

In response to the prime minister's inaction, a sense of frustration was building up among Goans in India as well as among the general public. His critics maintained that as long as Nehru was prime minister of India, Goa was safe for Portugal. Little hope was held for a voluntary change of colonial policy by Lisbon (Soares 1955), but after a revolt by anti-fascist forces on the Portuguese vessel *Santa Maria*, there was a widespread feeling among democrats that only a little effort by India was required to topple the Salazar regime in Lisbon.

The World Court Decision

It was not until August, in the midst of widespread revolt against Portuguese authority in Angola, that Nehru indicated a shift in his tactics towards Goa was possible. The opportunity to announce a change of course came about due to the consideration by Parliament of a bill to integrate Dadra and Nagar Haveli into the Indian Union. These enclaves, where Portuguese authority had been overthrown in 1954, were supposedly independent entities, but in reality had been governed by the Indian External Affairs Ministry. Portugal had filed an application with the International Court of Justice requesting it to declare that India had unlawfully prevented Lisbon from moving troops to Dadra and Nagar Haveli, thereby forcing it to lose the two possessions in the summer of 1954. Portugal further petitioned the Court to recognize Lisbon's sovereignty over the enclaves and declare that Indian forces should evacuate the occupied areas. Despite Indian objections, the case was tried.

In an ambiguous opinion the Court held that while Portugal had the right of passage before the occupation of the enclaves, it could not transport armed forces across Indian territory without New Delhi's permission. In addition, the Court stabilized the existing situation by deciding that since Portugal no longer controlled the enclaves, Lisbon no longer possessed the rights of passage it enjoyed before 1954 (*Case Concerning Right of Passage Over Indian Territory [Merits]*, Judgement of April 12, 1960: 6). Now, according to the Nehru government, the territories, which were supposedly independent entities, but in reality had been governed by the External Affairs Ministry in New Delhi, wanted officially to become part of the Indian Union.[57] To this end the Nehru government introduced legislation in Parliament to integrate Dadra and Nagar Haveli.

Nehru's August 1961 Speeches

It appears the Nehru government brought up the unfinished business of the former Portuguese colonies in order that it might introduce a new policy at a time when there was a widespread revolt in Angola. During the debate in the Rajya Sabha on August 16, the discussion immediately turned from Dadra and Nagar

Haveli to Goa. While defending his policy of not permitting *satya-grahis* to enter Goa, Nehru indicated—in what appeared to be a major policy shift—that when the time came he would send the army, not unarmed people. However, he claimed the situation was not yet appropriate for India to use its armed forces. The prime minister suggested that India's current pacific course had made a considerable impression all over the world when contrasted with Portuguese atrocities in Angola. Nevertheless, he declared that India's Goa policy 'cannot be considered a closed one.' He promised to give a good deal of thought 'as to whether we should vary our previous policy and, if so, in what way.'[58]

When pressed by the Communist leader Bhupesh Gupta, Nehru acknowledged his remarks constituted a change of policy. Clarifying his position the prime minister ruled out a sabotage campaign by stating that when the time came to send in the Indian army, 'it will be an open effort of ours and not a secret or furtive one.' Concluding his remarks, the aging leader indicated his own deep sense of frustration at the incompleteness of his revolution by exclaiming, 'I have no intention of passing away before Goa is liberated.'[59]

As if to reassure overjoyed Indians, while reminding the alarmed Portuguese that he meant business, Nehru reiterated his new outlook to the Lok Sabha the next day:

> The question of Goa as far as I can see, can only be dealt with either on a completely peaceful basis or on a fully armed basis. A time may come when you decide to deal with it on the armed basis. We will do so then . . . . If I am asked at the present moment to give any kind of assurance that we shall not use armed forces in regard to Goa, I am not prepared to give it. I do not know what we may do at any time, but we cannot at present, in regard to the development of events everywhere, rule out the question of using armed forces in regard to Goa.[60]

Afro-Asian Pressure

While most Indians were satisfied by his refusal to be bound by his commitment to peaceful means to settle the Goa dispute, Nehru learned at the Belgrade conference in September that other new nations required a great deal more from him. His restraint in Goa was being interpreted by a considerable segment of the world's people as a sign of weakness. He was accused of having lost his anti-colonial fervour by refusing to undertake the small effort needed to remove the Portuguese from India. Nehru had previously stated that whatever happened in Africa affected Goa.[61] The African leaders, reversing his words, claimed that whatever happened in Goa affected and made easier the African revolution (Fisher 1962: 9). They wanted an assurance that force would be employed as soon as possible against Portuguese possessions on the Indian subcontinent. The Chinese, who were not at Belgrade, unleashed a vicious campaign of abuse designed to undermine Nehru's leadership among the Afro-Asian states.[62] Beijing claimed that Indians were doing nothing to help the African cause but passing resolutions, while the Chinese were taking more active measures. Nehru left Belgrade with the recognition that he needed a new image. His pleas for peaceful coexistence, while much appreciated in the West, had created the impression in the rest of the world that India would never use force against the Portuguese in Goa. Deeply disturbed by the developments that had transpired in Yugoslavia, Nehru recognized that some instrument was now needed to rehabilitate India's image among the Afro-Asian nations.

However, New Delhi was reluctant to bring the Goa issue to the United Nations. Given its determination to prevent the international organization from conducting a plebiscite in Kashmir, India had always been reluctant to use the United Nations as a forum to settle its own disputes. In addition to its disdain for multilateral diplomacy (see A. Rubinoff 1991), India believed that taking the Goa issue to the UN would legally commit it to a peaceful settlement under the Charter. As Nehru's lieutenant V.K. Krishna Menon put it, 'Goa is not a subject we have brought up before the United Nations. It can be dealt with only in the general problem of colonialism' ('Portugal's Intervention in Goa': 107).

Against this background, India conducted a campaign in the United Nations General Assembly against Portuguese colonialism in Asia and Africa. This drive culminated on December 14 and 15, 1960 when the General Assembly labelled Goa a non-self governing territory. In doing so, it rejected Lisbon's contention that its metropolitan areas were an integral part of Portugal. At the same time Portugal was requested to provide information on the affairs of its colonies and report on Lisbon's efforts to assist them to independence.[63]

Months earlier, Nehru had expressed the opinion that 'the most horrible thing in the world today is what is happening in Angola.'[64] Nehru had linked developments in Africa with those on the sub-continent. According to him, 'Goa and Angola had become parts of a single problem—that of Portuguese colonialism' (Gopal 1984: 194). Yet very little had been done to coordinate India's efforts for Goa with the various struggles elsewhere against Portugal.

The opportunity to reestablish rapport with the other anti-colonial movements and focus attention on the alleged atrocities of Portuguese rule was provided by the Indian Council for Africa. Upon Prime Minister Nehru's return from Belgrade, it was announced that a four-day seminar on Portuguese colonialism would be held in New Delhi beginning October 20. The seminar, which also continued for a short time in Bombay, illustrates the transformation in Indian thinking when exposed to direct African pressure.[65] At the opening meeting in Delhi, Nehru stressed his familiar theme that India could not isolate any use of force in Goa from the use of force by the major powers in the context of the cold war. As at Belgrade, the prime minister stated that while colonialism was a cause of deep unrest, it was not responsible for all of the world's ills. The sole point which enthused his listeners was the promise that if 'some other steps' were necessary for its security, India would take them.[66] He assured his listeners, 'We are not in any sense tied down absolutely to pursuing the policy which we have thus far pursued in the interest of removal of colonialism. If we have to take some other action, we shall take it. We shall keep an open mind' (Nehru 1964: 367–68).

Less indication of a change in Indian policy was offered by Finance Minister Morarji Desai, one of the chief opponents of the use of force in the Nehru cabinet. In what was clearly the most unpopular address of the week, Desai acknowledged the right of Africans to use force in their struggle, but indicated that India could not take that course. In his opinion it was more important for India to be an example of non-violent policy than to take up arms against Portugal.[67]

As the seminar progressed, it became apparent that what had begun as a condemnation of Portuguese colonialism had become an attack upon India's Goa policy. The divergence between Indian and African positions was reflected in the desire of the latter for a joint military venture against Portugal. The African representatives made it plain they were not interested in mere pious resolutions, as they were involved in a bloody struggle with the Portuguese. What they wanted from India was more positive action. They maintained that the occupation of Goa by Indian forces would not be a small step in aiding their revolution. They asserted that once Goa fell the Portuguese Empire in Africa would collapse. They acknowledged they were presenting India with the opportunity to reassert its leadership and give the anti-colonial movement direction.

The African leaders issued India a challenge to choose between two tenets of its heritage. India was finally forced to choose whether it preferred its commitment to non-violent methods above its diminishing role as the leader of the anti-colonial struggle. Speaking for the African visitors, Kenneth Kaunda strongly urged India to reinforce its image in Africa. He noted that public opinion had not served to influence Western governments to assist in the solution of the Goa problem. In his view, India's policy of inaction in Goa abetted Portugal's repression in Africa.

What the Delhi sessions accomplished was to inform India that a substantial body of world opinion would support the use of force in Goa. Evidently, the Africans made their point, for when the sessions shifted to Bombay, a different attitude on the part of the host country could be discerned. The chairman of the reception committee, Y.B. Chavan, the chief minister of Maharashtra, noted the change in Indian mood when he said:

> I do not know how long even the Government of India will be able to resist the pressure of popular opinion and stand strictly by their principles . . . . Even at the cost of being considered passive by our friends in Africa, we have tried to observe the principles we have adopted. But it is impossible to watch the tremendous sacrifices of our friends in the Portuguese colonies in Africa as mere spectators and we will have to devise ways and means of preventing the extermination of a large number of people (Chavan 1961: 62–63).

Addressing a mass rally at Chowpatty beach, Prime Minister Nehru moved even further towards the African position. He frankly admitted that the policy pursued by the Government of India towards Portugal had been a failure. He announced that since Goa was a part of India, 'nothing' could prevent the completion of independence. Nehru said that recent events in Goa, such as cases of torture and a wave of terror, had compelled the government to do some fresh thinking and consider the problem anew. Amidst a thunderous ovation, he went on to explain, 'When I say I think afresh, I mean that we have been forced into thinking afresh by the Portuguese to adopt other methods to solve the problem. When and how I cannot say now. But I have no doubt that we will do it . . . .'[68]

The communiqué issued at the close of the seminar reflected the new Afro-Indian solidarity. It observed no efforts could be spared to bring about an end to Portuguese colonialism and no means eschewed to hasten it. The freedom of Goa was held to be of the greatest importance in the liberation of other countries and therefore a matter of special urgency to India as well as to the rest of the world community.[69]

The Invasion

After the October seminar, the official government attitude regarding Portuguese possessions on the subcontinent underwent profound change. Prime Minister Nehru's Chowpatty speech triggered increased accounts of terror and torture by Portuguese authorities in Goa. However, these reports by newspapers and politicians were necessarily restrained until Nehru returned from a state visit to Washington in November. As the prime minister went to persuade President Kennedy not to increase tensions with the Soviet Union, talk of an invasion of Goa by India was downplayed.

When Nehru returned home, it was announced that two incidents on November 17 and 24 had heightened Indo-Portuguese tensions. A shot fired from the Portuguese occupied island of Anjadev allegedly wounded a crew member of the *S.S. Sabarmati*. In the second incident a fisherman was said to have been killed in the same area off the coast of Karwar. In response, an independent member of Parliament called for an ultimatum ordering the Portuguese to leave Goa by Republic Day, January 26, 1962, or face the prospect of being thrown out by India. While acknowledging the incident as being a 'very important matter,' Prime Minister Nehru argued against this course. Characterizing the situation as developing, he preferred to see what transpired.[70]

What followed was an intense but often inaccurate and self-contradictory press campaign of pretense attributed to Defence Minister Krishna Menon and designed to make it appear as though Portugal were giving India provocation for an attack (Mankekar 1962: 22). This clumsy endeavour served to discredit India's position and obscured legitimate claims the country had to Goa. The daily press reported that Goa was an armed camp of 12,000 troops where roads were mined and bridges guarded.[71] The preposterous assertion that Radio Goa threatened to bomb Indian cities was advanced,[72] and the External Affairs Ministry claimed that Portuguese troops had raided a village inside the Indian border.[73]

The weekly press was even more spectacular in its 'coverage.' The leftist news magazine *Link* claimed that the Portuguese had hired foreign mercenaries 'with experience in methods of torture in Hitler's concentration camps . . . to work as guards and use their knowledge on Goan nationalists.'[74] A week later it described conditions inside Goa by asserting:

> The Goan Governor-General has declared a state of emergency. Dusk-to-dawn curfew has been clamped on most of the towns and bigger villages. Troop movements on the border have intensified. Inhabitants of almost all the border villages have been hurriedly packed off into the interior and the villages have been occupied by the troops. Such large-scale movement of population on short notice has been accompanied by mass arrests, flogging and locking up of people unable to comply with army orders.[75]

The validity of the Indian assertions regarding Portuguese aggressive activities was highly dubious and they were vehemently denied by Foreign Minister Franco Nogueira. It was most unlikely that Dr Salazar provoked his adversaries to attack what was an already precarious position.[76] Rather than engage in the actions attributed to them by the Indian press, the Portuguese instead invited international correspondents and other observers to come to Goa and 'examine the attitude of the forces present there and determine the nature and responsibility for any actions which may take place.'[77]

On the basis of what they saw, the journalists painted a far different picture than the one depicted by the Government of India. As Paul Grimes of the *New York Times* wrote, 'From inside Goa it appears inconceivable that the Portuguese would deliberately provoke an invasion.'[78] The Portuguese defenders, their ranks depleted by deployments to repress the rebellions in the African colonies of Angola and Mozambique, numbered less than the 3,500 military personnel that had been stationed in Goa in 1959. Those that remained constituted a force only large enough to put down an internal uprising, and there was no evidence of such a rebellion. It was not expected that this contingent could do battle with the Indian military more than ten times their number. Press reports contradicted charges of an imposed curfew and refuted the alleged military build up. No heavy armour or tanks could be found. Instead of the naval forces attributed to them, the Portuguese possessed only the aging frigate *Alfonso de Albuquerque* and one other smaller ship. What air force there was in the colonies was concerned with evacuating women and children by way of Karachi, Pakistan, not with strafing Indian territory. In order to assure that they would not be responsible for military contact, Portuguese forces withdrew from four strategic border positions.

Just as the Indian government circulated stories about alleged atrocities in Goa, so too did it make available information about Indian troop movements. The leading proponent of the use of force, in the Indian cabinet, Defence Minister V.K. Krishna Menon, claimed he decided not to impose press secrecy in order to give the Portuguese an opportunity to know the consequences of their actions.[79] Hence, the newspapers were filled with reports that over 100 passenger trains were cancelled in Bombay, Delhi, Punjab and other areas in order that troops might be moved to the Goa border. The Defence Ministry said it was 'dealing with the matter on the basis of a national emergency,'[80] while the Ministry of External Affairs claimed it necessary 'as a precautionary measure, to move certain armed forces to the areas threatened by aggressive manoeuvers.'[81]

Prime Minister Nehru, trapped by his own government's propaganda, had been forced to send a tri-service force 'on a scale that was lavish relative to [the] operational needs' of protecting Indian territory from alleged Portuguese incursions (Kavic 1967: 100).

Once in place, the army could not turn back without serious impairment of morale of the soldiers and a corresponding loss of confidence among the public. This situation created an atmosphere of militant anticipation that lasted for two weeks. The Portuguese had expected an attack as early as November 25.[82] Each day that it was delayed, added to the embarrassment of the Indian government and the impatience of Menon (Brecher 1968: 130). The longer the Indian army remained inactive, the more Prime Minister Nehru was subject to criticism by the Praja Socialist and Communist parties, which were urging immediate invasion. The Communist organ *New Age* chided, 'When is Prime Minister Nehru going to act? Will he remain a hero of empty words or act for Goan liberation and the unity of the Motherland?'[83]

Parliamentary inquiry came to a head during the foreign affairs debates in the Lok Sabha on December 7 and 8, and on December 11 in the Rajya Sabha. However, Prime Minister Nehru still refused to be pinned down to any definite course of action. He declared, as the situation was a developing one, the government was 'preparing for any contingency that may arise,' even though he could not outline the 'precise steps to be taken.'[84] Nevertheless, each House gave its approval for a foreign policy that remained unrevealed to it. To the very end Nehru remained characteristically ambivalent about whether he would use force. Although he told the Rajya Sabha 'our patience is certainly exhausted,'[85] the prime minister promised the Lok Sabha he had not closed the door to the peaceful settlement of the dispute.[86]

While the delay was partly due to logistical difficulties in moving troops, it was also attributable to the considerable diplomatic activity that had been going on during the fortnight prior to the invasion. On December 8, using the Brazilian government as an intermediary, Portugal proposed to demonstrate its peaceful intentions by offering to send independent observers to the border. India, in its reply, made through the United Arab Republic, suggested that Portugal vacate Goa 'forthwith'.[87] When the alarmed Portuguese called the attention of the United Nations to the Indian build up on December 11, New Delhi claimed its dispatch of reinforcements to be a precautionary measure. Acting Secretary General U Thant sent messages to Dr Salazar and Nehru on December 15 exhorting them to ensure that the situation did not deteriorate into a threat to peace. He urged immediate negotiations leading to an early solution of the problem in accordance with the principles embodied in the United Nations charter. In response, Dr Salazar offered to provide India guarantees that Portugal's Asian possessions would never be used against its security interests. He stated that negotiations for such an agreement 'can take place where and how the Government in New Delhi may wish.'[88] In his reply Nehru said it was impossible to negotiate in accordance with the principles of the United Nations with a country that repeatedly ignored the international organization's declarations on colonialism. He noted that for fourteen years Portugal had steadfastly refused to discuss yielding sovereignty in Goa.

Other attempts at moving India towards talks with Portugal were made by Sir Paul Gore-Booth, the United Kingdom's high commissioner in Delhi and Ambassador John Kenneth Galbraith of the United States, but both fell short of formal mediation. Ambassador Galbraith, who managed to postpone the invasion twice could offer only vague guarantees of American pressure on Portugal in exchange for a six month standstill—not specific assurances that the United States could get its Portuguese ally out of Goa (Galbraith 1969: Chapter XIV, p. 284; and U.S. Department of State 1994: 908–21).

By this time it was obvious that the Nehru government was now committed to the use of force to bring Goa into the Indian Union. The cabinet had met to consider the crisis on December 6, and eight days later a top level military conference of the Chiefs of Staff of the army and the airforce was held at the border town of Belgaum. Sensing the inevitable, the United States and Great Britain made it clear they would not become involved in any hostilities.

Finally at midnight on December 17–18, the uncertainty of several weeks was ended and Operation Vijay finally commenced. Thirty thousand Indian soldiers, under the overall command of Lieutenant-General N.N. Chaudhuri and the field direction of Major General Kenneth Candeth poured into Goa, Daman and Diu. General Thaper, Chief of Army Staff, told his troops, 'You are not going into Goa as conquerors but protectors.'[89]

As the Indians anticipated, the evacuation of Portuguese officials led to the swift collapse of the colonial regime (Khera 1974). Despite their pledge to fight to the last man, the Portuguese offered virtually no resistance in most areas. Casualties were light, with only between thirty-nine and seventy-five killed, and within thirty-six hours all opposition was overcome. Instead of the 12,500 troops they asserted opposed them, the Indians took only 3,500 prisoners.

After the invasion Prime Minister Nehru claimed India derived no satisfaction from taking armed action, but he declared, 'The Portuguese ultimately left no choice open to us.'[90] According to him Indian troops had been instructed to employ a minimum amount of force and 'the very swiftness of the end and the very few casualties on either side showed the correctness of the Indian assessment.'[91]

Reaction

International

Pressure from Portugal's allies had failed to deter India from taking action in Goa. However, immediately after the outbreak of hostilities, Portugal attempted to persuade the United Nations Security Council to order a cease-fire; withdrawal of Indian troops to their original positions; and engagement of India in diplomatic discussions. Accordingly, the United States introduced a resolution for these steps to be taken in that sequence.[92] The vote was indicative of world reaction. The proposal was favoured by Portugal's NATO allies: the United States, United Kingdom, France, and Turkey as well as the American controlled delegations from Nationalist China, Ecuador and Chile. In opposition stood the Afro-Asian states: Ceylon, Liberia and the United Arab Republic. They were supported by the Soviet Union, which by the exercise of its permanent member's veto sustained India's position. Although a counter-resolution calling on Portugal to terminate hostile action and cooperate with India on the liquidation of its colonial possessions failed, Portugal's allies did not attempt to bring the matter to the General Assembly. However, on the very next day, December 19, Portugal was condemned by that body for non-compliance with the earlier order to report on activities in its colonies.[93] The vote provided overwhelming evidence that had the Goa problem reached the General Assembly, the Indian viewpoint supported by the huge Afro-Asian delegation would have prevailed.

Significantly, it was the United States that took the lead in advancing Portugal's argument. Under pressure from Dr Salazar, the Kennedy administration—heretofore regarded as being sympathetic to India on the matter—decided to focus on the narrow point of aggression and not raise the issue of colonialism in Goa. More revealingly, American officials were elated over the prospect of serving the Indian prime minister a dose of the same medicine he had been giving them since independence. According to Arthur Schlesinger (1965: 527):

> . . . the contrast between Nehru's incessant sanctimony on the subject of non-aggression and his brisk exercise of *Machtpolitik* was too comic not to cause comment. It was a little like catching the preacher in the hen house; and it suggested that Harrow and Cambridge, in instilling the British virtues, had not neglected hypocrisy. If such judgments were unfair, it was almost too much to expect the targets of Nehru's past sermons not to respond in kind.

While not unfavourable in private to the merits of India's position, the American delegate to the United Nations Adlai Stevenson carried the attitude of ridicule to the extreme. He began by recalling with respect to India that, 'Few nations have done more to uphold the principles of this Organization or to support its peace-making efforts all over the world, and none have espoused non-violence more vehemently and invoked the peaceful symbolism of Gandhi more frequently.' He went on to add that only recently had Nehru, the 'lifelong disciple of one of the world's great saints of peace, whom many have looked up to as an apostle of non-violence,' addressed the international organization on the importance of pacific settlement of disputes. Yet he noted that at this very moment the Indian Minister of Defence, V.K. Krishna Menon, 'so well known in these halls for his advice on matters of peace and his tireless enjoinders to everyone else to seek the way of compromise, was on the borders of Goa inspecting his troops at the zero hour of invasion.' Stevenson concluded his remarks in terms conspicuously similar to those employed by India in 1947 when New Delhi denounced Dutch actions in Indonesia, by claiming that just as the failure of its members to prevent the use of force was responsible for the death of the League of Nations, now the effectiveness of the United Nations was imperilled because of India's attack on Goa. He eulogized, 'Tonight we are witnessing the first act in a drama which could end with [the United Nations'] death.'[94]

Similar criticism came from virtually every Western government.[95] Especially vocal was the British foreign secretary, Lord Hume, who assailed those Security Council members who voted against the cease-fire resolution.[96] Apparently, Goa crystallized misgivings many countries had built up toward India and the neutralist policies of its leader. It is interesting to note how the issue was clothed in personal terms and centred on Nehru rather than on the merits of the dispute. While this hostility was true of governmental reactions, it was even more pronounced in the Western press. Conservative publications took great delight in pointing out that Nehru's India was capable of operating in the same manner as most other states. Representative of this school of journalism was the English publication *Spectator* which claimed that

> . . . although there is a good deal to be said against Portugal, there is nothing whatever to be said in favour of India . . . . The fact remains that India—the India of Mr Nehru—has committed an act of aggression, bolstering it with all the usual phrases and excuses that aggressors have used in recent decades[97] ('Mr Nehru's Adventure' 1961: 920).

Nor was the opinion of moderate journals much different. Even those publications like the *New York Times* that supported India's claim to Goa, disapproved of its method of acquisition. They felt that India's role in the cause of world peace, so often exercised in the past, would never again be free of the stain of the use of force in Goa. Typical of this range of opinion, the *Economist* commented, 'All allowances made, it is a sad day for the friends of world peace, freedom and law who had grown used to India as a natural ally and Mr Nehru as their spokesman.'[98]

The barrage of criticism that the occupation of Goa brought forth in Europe and the Americas surprised the Indians and embittered Nehru. He was particularly incensed that for years both the United States and Great Britain had refused to persuade their Portuguese ally to vacate Goa, only to become interested in the problem at the last moment. The Indians claimed that they were victims of a double standard, applied to them by the West to which, they argued, no other country would have been subjected for a similar action. They resented those who on the one hand urged non-violence in dealing with Portugal in Goa, while encouraging India to use force against China in the Himalayas (see B.K. Nehru 1962). Yet in light of India's past behaviour, one cannot help wondering what would have been India's reaction if another country had used force before exhausting all peaceful methods in a similar situation.

So far as Nehru was concerned, he maintained, 'In spite of the fact that I have been called a hypocrite, I might say I work for peace.' He did not appreciate being accorded a position of world leadership which a perennially hostile section of the Western press had never before been inclined to grant him. The prime minister remarked, 'I am preached non-violence by people who have no right to say anything about it, nor have any conception of it.'[99]

The disapproval voiced in the Western world over India's use of force in Goa can be contrasted with the enthusiasm expressed by the Afro-Asian states. Except for India's arch foe Pakistan, which viewed the action as 'naked militarism,'[100] and China, which offered qualified praise,[101] hardly any dissent could be found in the two continents that were usually the first to decry the use of force by the major powers.

Similarly, virtually all communist countries—and especially the Soviet Union—voiced their enthusiastic approval of the Indian action. Taking full advantage of the opportunity to connect the United States with its Portuguese ally, Moscow Radio declared, 'The attitude toward the struggle of India for the liberation of Goa clearly shows who is for and who is against colonialism, who are the friends and who are enemies of the peoples of Asia and Africa.'[102] In almost identical language Indian communists profitably gained by comparing and contrasting positions of the United States and the Soviet Union in the matter.[103] To show his gratitude for Russian support, Prime Minister Nehru acknowledged, 'the Soviet Union appreciated our stand and action. We thank them for it.'[104] Such mutual expressions of affinity caused Portugal's foreign minister, Franco Nogueira, to assert that India was now 'absolutely identified with the Soviet Russia.'[105] Thus despite years of effort by India to prevent such an occurrence, Goa had become a cold war issue.

India

In India virtually all political parties and major newspapers endorsed the forceful incorporation of Goa into the Union, even if they expressed reservations about the timing which was less compelling than after so many *satyagrahis* had been killed in 1955. Typical was the reaction of *The Hindustan Times*, which saluted the government for the swiftness of the occupation as well as the small loss of life.[106] While former governor-general, Chakravarti Rajagopala-chari, castigated Nehru for violating Gandhian principles,[107] other commentators criticized the government for unnecessarily fabricating a pretext for invasion.[108] Nevertheless, the military operation in the Portuguese colonies served to provide a great surge of renewed popular support for the regime's foreign policy. According to an armed forces publication, 'Nothing in the post-independence history of Indian armed forces had been so brilliant and impressive on the minds of the people' (Singh 1962: 821).[109] A public opinion poll revealed that only three per cent of the population felt that military action should not have been employed to integrate Goa into the country.[110] At the same time the government's show of force deprived the opposition parties of one of their main targets of criticism. Most opposition spokesmen were content to point to the obvious truth that the Nehru government's past failures in Goa had finally forced India to resort to the more militant methods they had long advocated. As the Jan Sangh party's organ commented, Nehru's indecisiveness had complicated an essentially simple problem to the extent that the price paid ultimately outweighed what was gained.[111]

Ironically India's annexation of Goa by military means, which temporarily estranged it from the West, did not serve to stem the decline of New Delhi's influence in the Afro-Asian world to deter China from attacking within a year. Nor did it bring down the Salazar government in Portugal or directly assist the freedom struggles in the African colonies of Angola, Portuguese Guinea, and Mozambique. Yet, at least Indians had the satisfaction of knowing that the last European colonial outpost on the subcontinent was no longer under the control of a foreign government.

Problems of Transition

The conquest of the Portuguese possessions did not mean the end of Goa as an issue in Indian politics, as almost immediately Goa became the object of national absorption. Even though India took only two days to militarily overrun the Portuguese possessions, New Delhi was not at the time prepared to administer them. An American diplomatic communication warned, 'The Government of India will have to give special attention to the economic development of Goa so as to make the people feel that they are at least as well off as they were under the Portuguese.'[112] However, the ensuing inefficiency and declining standard of living in the former colonies initially inhibited their integration. As one Goan writer complained:

No one seems to realize that Goa was liberated in order to remove the last vestige of foreign domination in India, to make its people masters of their own household and to afford them an opportunity to develop their own way of life as free citizens of independent India. No sooner was the political domination of Goa by the Portuguese brought to an end than began calculated well-planned maneuvers by some politicians to deprive them of their legitimate rights and aspirations and impose on them a political set-up which is not of their choosing (Esteves 1966: vi).

The Nehru government, sensitive to charges that it was replacing one type of imperialism with another, proceeded cautiously towards political integration. Military rule, designed to restore normal life and communications in the liberated territories, lasted six months. Not until June 8, 1962 did a civilian governor take office. In the meantime the Twelfth Amendment Act of 1962 conferred union territory status retroactively from December 20 of the previous year. Simultaneously with the constitutional amendment, the Goa, Daman and Diu Administration Act provided representation of the territories in Parliament. In August the lieutenant governor appointed an informal advisory Consultative Council consisting of twenty-nine nominated members to assist in the administration of the territory (Study Team on Administration of Union Territories and NEFA 1968: 173). In that same month, two well known physicians representing each major religious community, Dr Pundalik Gaitonde, a Hindu from North Goa, and Dr Antonio Colaco, a Christian from South Goa, were appointed by Prime Minister Nehru to represent the territory in the Lok Sabha. The transition to popular government accelerated when panchayat elections were held in October 1962 and an impressive sixty-two per cent of the populace exercised their franchise in contests that were not fought along party lines. In accordance with provisions of the Fourteenth Amendment Act of 1962, the Government of Union Territories Act of 1963 established a thirty member legislative assembly.

Yet, it was 'an irony of post-liberation Goa'[113] that the expression of political freedom was accompanied by 'a host of economic and administrative problems' (National Council of Applied Economic Research 1964: 19). Among the hardships that materialized were those that resulted from the shift in legal systems and the language of government. The importation of deputized civil servants from neighbouring Indian states was particularly resented by the local populace. However, the most serious situation in this period was the decline in the standard of living for the average Goan. Prior to its annexation, salaries had been higher in Goa, and prices lower when compared with the Indian Union. Moreover, as Goa had been a centre of smuggling activities before 1961, foreign goods had been accessible and cheap. Incorporation into India resulted in a price rise of between thirty to fifty per cent on most items and scarcities of what had come to be regarded as essential commodities. It also meant the gradual imposition of Indian taxes and liquor laws. Since 'Goans had been used to low customs duties on imported articles and consumption of these had come to be identified in their minds with their own personality,' for many residents of the former Portuguese colonies on the subcontinent integration initially came to be equated with 'despair' (Ribeiro 1966: 77).

END NOTES

1. Shadi (1962) discusses the unsuccessful efforts of the Praja Socialist and Communist parties, as well as the various Goan liberation groups, to pressure the Government of India to take a stronger stand and invade Goa.
2. *New York Times*, October 2, 1951, p. 5.
3. *Lok Sabha Debates*, Second Series, November 24, 1961, Vol. LIX, No. 4, column 1125. Alva claimed he asked Sir Stafford Cripps, the English negotiator, what the attitude of Great Britain would be in regard to Goa after India attained independence. Cripps shrugged his shoulders and said that would have to be a matter for the future Government of India to deal with.

4. *New York Times*, June 5, 1952, p. 4.
5. Ibid., December 22, 1955, p. 8.
6. Ibid., August 15, 1950, p. 4, and Parthasarathi (1986: 28).
7. Ibid., June 11, 1953, p. 3.
8. Ibid., July 12, 1953, p. 20.
9. Ibid., March 27, 1954, p. 2
10. Ibid., June 27, 1954, p. 5.
11. Ibid., July 23, 1954, p. 1.
12. Ibid., July 26, 1954, p. 2.
13. Ibid., July 29, 1954, p. 6.
14. Ibid., July 31, 1954, p. 2.
15. Ibid., August 8, 1954, p. 14.
16. Ibid., August 14, 1954, p. 5.
17. Ibid., August 16, 1954, p. 4.
18. There was fear that Pakistan would send *satyagrahis* into Kashmir if the method were transposed into the international sphere.
19. *Keesing's Contemporary Archives*, 1955, p. 14274.
20. *New York Times*, August 17, 1954, p. 1.
21. *Keesing's Contemporary Archives*, 1955, pp. 14275–76.
22. *Hindustan Overseas Times* (New Delhi), June 2, 1955, p. 1.
23. Ibid., June 9, 1955, p. 2.
24. Ibid., p. 4.
25. *New York Times*, July 26, 1955, p. 16.
26. Ibid., p. 1 and p. 3.
27. *New York Times*, August 13, 1955, p. 3.
28. 'Goa Blunders,' *Economist*, August 20, 1955, p. 602.
29. *New Age*, August 28, 1955, p. 1.
30. *New York Times*, August 20, 1955, p. 6. Egypt, which had no consul in Goa, represented India through its mission in Lisbon, while Brazil agreed to look after Portuguese interests in India.
31. *Keesing's Contemporary Archives*, 1955, p. 14402.
32. The *Economist* quipped, 'The Goa season . . . is now quite an established international divertissement for the otherwise dull month of August.' 'Goa in the News Again,' *Economist*, August 20, 1955, p. 461.
33. *New York Times*, April 4, 1958, p. 4.
34. Ibid., June 7, 1958, p. 39.
35. *Lok Sabha Debates*, Second Series, Vol. LI, No. 11, February 28, 1961, column 2080.
36. Ibid., Vol. LIII, No. 34, April 1, 1961, column 8474.
37. Ibid., Vol. LIX, November 20, 1961, column 103.
38. See *New York Times*, September 17, 1955, p. 6.
39. See the British note in which Portugal is referred to in this language. *New York Times*, August 7, 1954, p. 2.
40. *New York Times*, April 13, 1954, p. 2.
41. Cf. after the invasion of Goa the British claimed they had informed Lisbon in 1954 that their country would not engage in hostilities with another member of the Commonwealth on behalf of Portugal. *New York Times*, January 4, 1962, p. 12.

42. *New York Times*, September 3, 1954, p. 3.
43. Ibid., July 1, 1961, p. 4.
44. *The Hindu* (Madras), June 19, 1961, p. 1.
45. *New York Times*, November 3, 1953, p. 4.
46. *Hindustan Overseas Times* (New Delhi), September 15, 1955, p. 12.
47. *New York Times*, December 3, 1955, p. 3.
48. 'U.S.–Portuguese Conversations, Text of Joint Communiqué,' *U.S. Department of State Bulletin*, XXXIII (December 12, 1955), p. 967.
49. *New York Times*, December 5, 1955, p. 1.
50. 'Excerpts from Transcript of Secretary Dulles' News Conference,' *U.S. Department of State Bulletin*, XXXIII (December 19, 1955), p. 1007.
51. *New York Times*, December 8, 1955, p. 25.
52. Ibid., January 13, 1956, p. 2.
53. Ibid., February 16, 1956, p. 2.
54. *Congress Bulletin, 1961*, Nos. 3–6 (March–June), p. 252.
55. Years before he was famous for the remark that neutralism was immoral (John Foster Dulles, 'The Cost of Peace,' *U.S. Department of State Bulletin*, XXXIV, June 18, 1956, p. 1000), Dulles was already unpopular in India for a statement made in January, 1947 linking the new Congress government to the Soviet Union. *New York Times*, January 21, 1947, p. 11.
56. 'Prime Minister's Statement Initiating Rajya Sabha Debates,' *Foreign Affairs Record* VI (December 1960), p. 434.
57. Interestingly, Dadra and Nagar Haveli have remained union territories, with their own representation in the Lok Sabha, and have not become part of Gujarat state.
58. *Rajya Sabha Debates*, Vol. XXXV, No. 2, August 16, 1961, column 386.
59. Ibid., column 399.
60. *Lok Sabha Debates*, Second Series, Vol. LXVI, No. 8, August 17, 1961, columns 2774–75.
61. *Congress Bulletin, 1961*, Nos 3–6 (March–June), p. 252.
62. See *The Hindu* (Madras), September 5, 1961, p. 1.
63. United Nations General Assembly, *Official Records*, 947th and 948th Meetings, December 14 and 15, 1960.
64. *New York Times*, July 1, 1961, p. 4.
65. Among those leaders attending the conference were Kenneth Kaunda of Northern Rhodesia; Mgilo Sivai, Minister for Commerce and Industry of Tanganyika; Abdel Karimel-Khatib, Minister for African Affairs of Morocco; Thomas R. Khanja of the Congo; Augustine Signando from Southern Rhodesia; Alfredo Pereira of Portuguese Guinea; Marcellino Dos Santos and Adelino Gwande of Mozambique; Joad Cabral of the Goa League, London; and Wedgewood Benn, Committee for the Liberation of Portuguese Colonies, also of London. See *The Hindu* (Madras), September 21, 1961, p. 1.
66. *New York Times*, October 21, 1961, p. 1 and p. 8.
67. *The Hindu* (Madras), October 23, 1961, p. 1.
68. Ibid., October 24, 1961.
69. Ibid., October 25, 1961, p. 1.
70. Ibid., November 25, 1961, p. 1.
71. Ibid., December 5, 1961.
72. Ibid., December 6, 1961, p. 1.

73. *New York Times*, December 11, 1961, p. 3.
74. 'Goa Liberation,' *Link*, December 3, 1961, p. 8.
75. 'Provocation in Goa,' *Link*, December 10, 1961, p. 6.
76. When I asked Mr. Menon, the former defence minister, why the Portuguese would go out of their way to give the Indians a pretext to resort to arms, he replied, 'I don't know.' Interview, New Delhi, January 11, 1969.
77. *New York Times*, December 9, 1961, p. 6.
78. Ibid., December 16, 1961, p. 10. For a description of actual conditions in Goa see that paper's coverage on December 12, 1961, p. 1, p. 15 and p. 19; December 13, 1961, p. 4; December 15, 1961, p. 10 and December 16, 1961, p. 10.
79. *The Hindu* (Madras), December 11, 1961, p. 8.
80. Ibid., December 5, 1961, p. 1.
81. Ibid., December 6, 1961, p. 1.
82. *New York Times*, November 27, 1961, p. 1.
83. *New Age*, November 19, 1961, p. 1.
84. *Lok Sabha Debates*, Vol. LX, No. 15, December 7, 1961, Column 3863.
85. *Rajya Sabha Debates*, Vol. XXXVI, December 11, 1961, Column 1776.
86. *Lok Sabha Debates*, Vol. LX, No. 16, December 8, 1961, Column 4264.
87. *Keesing's Contemporary Archives*, 1962, p. 18636.
88. *New York Times*, December 18, 1961, p. 10.
89. *The Hindu* (Madras), December 18, 1961, p. 1 and p. 8.
90. *New York Times*, December 19, 1961, p. 1.
91. Ibid., December 20, 1961, p. 1.
92. See United Nations Security Council, *Official Records*, 987th and 988th Meetings, December 18, 1961.
93. See United Nations General Assembly, *Official Records*, 1083rd Meeting, December 19, 1961.
94. 'Security Council Considers Situation in Goa,' *U.S. Department of State Bulletin*, XLVI (January 22, 1962), p. 145, p. 149.
95. See the *New York Times*, December 19, 1961, p. 16 for a survey of official reaction.
96. Ibid., December 29, 1961, p. 1 and p. 3.
97. For further examples of this line of thought see National Secretariat for Information 1962.
98. 'Fallen Idol', *Economist*, December 23, 1961, p. 1198.
99. *New York Times*, December, 29, 1961, p. 3.
100. Ibid., December 19, 1961, p. 16.
101. The Chinese claimed India's only motive in seizing Goa was to recover sagging prestige among the Afro-Asians. *New York Times*, December 20, 1961, p. 2.
102. *New York Times*, December 19, 1961, p. 15.
103. See Gupta (1962: 12 *et passim*); and *New Age*, December 24, 1961.
104. *New York Times*, December 28, 1961, p. 1.
105. Ibid., December 22, 1961, p. 3.
106. *The Hindustan Times* (New Delhi), December 19, 1961.
107. C.R., 'Dear Reader,' *Swarajya* VI, December 30, 1961, p. 9 and January 6, 1962, p. 11.

108. A.D. Gorwala (1961: 15–16) felt the merits of India's case justified the invasion.

109. Jaswant Singh, ed., *Indian Armed Forces Yearbook 1961–1962* (Bombay, 1962), p. 851.

110. Indian Institute of Public Opinion, *Monthly Public Opinion Survey*, October–November, 1962, p. 58.

111. *Organiser*, December 18, 1961, p. 1.

112. 'American Consulate Bombay to Department of State,' March 28, 1962, State Department Central Files, 1853d00/3-2862.

113. *The Times of India* (New Delhi), April 23, 1963.

Chapter 4

The Communal Pattern of Politics

◆

The territorial integration of Goa, Daman and Diu did not resolve the place of the former Portuguese colonies in India. Goa's future status now became the principal issue to dominate territorial politics after the departure of Portugal. Three possible options—independence, union territory status and statehood—initially presented themselves, while a fourth alternative—merger with Maharashtra—soon followed. Significantly, reaction to these alternatives polarized along communal lines. In situations where democratic politics begin in a vacuum, as was the case in Goa, the emergence of communally-based issues becomes an integral part of the political landscape. There is an incentive for political parties to organize on a sectarian basis, and voters respond to the mutual incompatibility of communal claims to power. The reliance on such issues is, therefore, a calculated strategy by leaders in the majority community to produce electoral success (see Tambiah 1996: 330). As Donald Horowitz (1985: 294–95) suggests, such issues offer political leaders the promise of a secure basis of support, but lead to ascriptive fixidity as minority groups respond accordingly. Interestingly, Christians appropriated Goan identity, but advocated statehood within the Indian Union as a more secure means of protecting their culture within a larger political community.

Based on what they claimed were distinctive historical, social, and cultural patterns, some Goans made a futile plea for independence before the United Nations (see *Goa Petitioners in the United Nations* 1964), while others unsuccessfully challenged Indian sovereignty in the courts.[1] As a result of these developments, the successful integration of the Christian community was of special concern to the Indian government. As far back as August 25, 1954, Prime Minister Nehru—a life long advocate of a secular state— had sought to reassure Goan Christians that their right to practice their religion would be guaranteed under the Indian constitution (J. Nehru 1958b: 375). Even before its incorporation into the Indian Union, Nehru had committed his country to respect Goan autonomy.[2] At a public meeting in Panjim on May 22, 1963, in his only visit to the former Portuguese colonies after liberation, Nehru recognized Goa's 'distinctive personality' which he felt entitled it to remain a 'separate entity' within India's federal system (J. Nehru 1968: 58). Significantly, in moving the bill which gave Goa union territory status on March 14, 1962, Nehru pledged that India would maintain the area's 'separate identity' which he asserted had evolved through 400 years of history (J. Nehru 1964: 45). While statehood was deemed out of the question until integration was assured through economic assistance provided by the centre, the Government of India indicated that it did not prefer to see Goa absorbed into a neighbouring state so soon after its incorporation.[3] As Mrs Lakshmi Menon, the deputy minister of external affairs told Parliament, 'One reason we have decided to keep Goa as a union territory is the rival pulls of Maharashtra and other states which want to make Goa a part of them.'[4]

Nevertheless, both Maharashtra and Mysore, already in dispute over Belgaum, embarked on a campaign to digest Goa, which was economically more prosperous than their respective border areas.[5] Many Hindu Goans supported these endeavours, for they regarded merger with an adjoining state to be an effective means of promoting national integration. They considered Portuguese rule to be an 'accident of history' (Priolkar 1967: 46), and denied that Goans were in any way distinguishable from people in neighbouring states. As many freedom fighters had operated from Maharashtra in the pre-liberation period (see Kunte 1978), they shared a desire to see Goa as a district in that state. In the process of fighting foreign rule, they had formed close political ties with such Maharashtra politicians as Y.B. Chavan, S.M. Joshi and Nath Pai, who as advocates of linguistic states later encouraged Goans to push for merger with Maharashtra.[6] While the merger proposal lay dormant until liberation, it became the principal issue of the 1963 elections.

The Merger Issue

In March of 1963, advocates of merger founded the Maharashtra-wadi Gomantak Party (MGP) whose 'object [was] the integration of Goa into the state of Maharashtra.' The organization further believed 'the language of Goans is Marathi and [claimed] Konkani is a dialect of Marathi.' It also considered Goa to be 'historically and geographically, culturally and economically, part and parcel of Maharashtra.'[7] As a result of its ties to Indian politicians and political parties in Maharashtra, the MGP had at its disposal sufficient resources to mount an intensive campaign. The MGP issued no manifesto. It merely asserted that since its only purpose was to secure the merger of Goa with Maharashtra, the party would be dissolved when that objective was achieved (Esteves 1986: 75).

In reaction, the primarily Konkani-speaking Christian minority, which had dominated the colony under the Portuguese, founded the United Goans Party (UGP or UG) in September 1963 to prevent the dilution of their community's distinct culture and language. The UGP was a product of the merger of four embryonic organizations: the Goencho Paksh; the Partido Indiano; the Goan National Union and the United Front of Goans which traced its roots back to 1950 (Halappa et al. 1964: 45). The founder-president of the Goencho Paksh, Dr Jack Sequeira was chosen president of the new party. Compared to the financial resources at the disposal of the MGP, the United Goans had 'no elaborate bureaucratic apparatus for campaigning' (ibid.: 53).

Despite the evident political activity that was transpiring in Goa, the Congress party, confident that it would sweep the polls in the territory's first general elections as had been the case elsewhere in India, waited until September 1962 to organize. At that time Purshottam Kakodkar, a prominent freedom fighter but an inept politician, was chosen as president of the local organization. Although the Congress was without historical roots in Goa, the party still expected to capitalize on post-liberation sentiment as it had done throughout British India. Yet, by stressing its all-India identity, the Congress instead bore the brunt of the problems associated with transition. Although a victim of circumstances with regard to these matters, Congress officials made strategic blunders that damaged the party's future prospects. Instead of building a cohesive grassroots organization of like-minded people, the Congress in Goa tried to replicate the umbrella pattern of the all-India party. It absorbed most of the disparate liberation groups without regard to their ideological persuasion and in the process created a legacy of indiscipline that was to last a generation. As one analyst described the situation, 'Everyone who claimed to be a Congressman was welcomed into the organization without [knowledge of] what his or her views were on some of the problems facing political parties in Goa at that time' (Esteves 1971: 144).[8] As a consequence of being run by political exiles appointed from Delhi, the party was oblivious to local issues that were bound to emerge in the territorial elections scheduled for December 1963. It was unable to release its seventeen point election manifesto until the first week of October.

The response of the Congress to the merger issue was complicated by its position as a national party, specifically the rivalry of its Maharashtra and Mysore wings. In reaction to Maharashtra's expansionist claims which were expressed in legislative resolutions, Mysore advanced its own declaration of merger which also was based on economic and linguistic ties.[9] As both states had Congress governments and strong leaders in Y.B. Chavan and S.N. Nijalingappa, the national party was in a stalemate when it was called upon to take an electoral stand on Goa's future status.

The Congress Party's Debacle in the 1963 Elections

Caught on the horns of a dilemma when it came to the allocation of tickets for the 1963 campaign, the local Congress tried to maintain that the future of Goa was not an election issue. Falling between two stools, it could not placate either side of the merger issue and suffered the resignation of many prominent members as a result. Not until one month before the December elections did the Congress finalize its list of candidates. The outcome heavily favoured the status quo forces. Of the twenty-eight candidates nominated by the Congress in Goa proper, not more than ten favoured the immediate merger of the territory with Maharashtra (Joshi 1964: 1097). The split personality of the Congress was exacerbated by a parade of prominent outside political figures such as Lal Bahadur Shastri and Y.B. Chavan who respectively advocated a continuation of union territory status or endorsed merger with Maharashtra.

Just as the Indian National Congress had naturally considered anti-colonial activity to be a requisite for granting a ticket, so too did the Congress party in Goa feel compelled to select freedom fighters as its candidates. As a consequence, its list was predominantly Hindu Brahmans, since that community had dominated the resistance to Portuguese rule. Thus, only six of the eighteen Hindus given tickets by the Congress were non-Brahmans, even though they constituted ninety per cent of the non-Christian population. Disenchanted Congressmen who had been advocates of the merger were driven into the MGP, which formed an alliance with the Praja Socialist Party. The Congress' criteria for the selection of the candidates was a recipe for disaster, for it enabled Goa's first free election to be fought on caste and communal lines. The electoral symbol of the MGP was the 'lion' associated with Shivaji and the symbol of the UGP was the 'hand' associated with St Francis Xavier. In a campaign waged on that basis among unsophisticated voters, the advantage was certain to go to the MGP. Its core supporters being rural illiterates, who believed that they had been exploited by their higher caste co-religionists as well as the Christians during the centuries of Portuguese rule, the MGP promised land-to-the-tiller reforms. As a non-Brahman Hindu-oriented party, the MGP was able to mobilize both anti-Brahman and anti-Catholic sentiments among its numerically superior constituency of voters. It alleged that if the United Goans came to power, they would work for a return of Portuguese rule and revive Hindu suppression (Halappa et al. 1964: 108).

As a result of the inability of the Congress to reach a solution satisfactory to both Hindus and Catholics, an opening had been given to the MG and UG parties which pressed respectively for the extremes of merger with Maharashtra and statehood. Drawing its strength from the predominantly Hindu New Conquest outlying regions which had become Portuguese in the late eighteenth century, the MGP and its allies garnered over forty per cent of the popular vote and won sixteen Assembly seats and in cooperation with the Praja Socialist Party captured both parliamentary constituencies. In reaction to what they regarded as a threat to the region's separate identity, the Christian community coalesced around the United Goans. The UG, whose support was concentrated in the Old Conquest coastal *talukas*, secured just under thirty per cent of the popular vote and picked up twelve Assembly seats. An independent was returned from Diu, while the only Congressman who secured election to the territorial legislature came from Daman. Although it fielded twenty-nine candidates, the Congress party received less than seventeen per cent of the popular vote (Table 4.1).

Table 4.1
Results of the 1963 Assembly Elections

Party	Candidates	Valid Votes	Percentage	Seats
MG	27	100,179	40.13	16
UG	24	74,081	29.68	12
INC	29	41,727	16.72	1
Others	69	30,611	13.48	1
Total	149	246,598 out of 350,032 eligible	70.45	30

Source: *Assembly Elections Ready Reference 1994: 26.*

The results of the 1963 Goa elections were described 'as the most serious electoral debacle' the Congress party had suffered up to that point.[10] Its ideology of secularism had clashed with existing primordial loyalties which were exacerbated by the impact of democratic politics and modernization in a post-colonial setting. The communal nature of the results 'pained' Prime Minister Nehru in particular.[11] Yet, until the question of merger was resolved, there could be no place in Goa for a national political party that stressed economic issues and relied on appearances by central cabinet ministers as a substitute for mass appeal. The communal pattern was thus established in Goan politics for the next decade, for as Horowitz (1985: 346) affirms, the ethnic politics axis preempts other issues from emerging. Hence, until the question of merger was resolved, no comprehensive programme for the territory's economic development was possible.

The Opinion Poll

With the election of the MGP under the leadership of Chief Minister Dayand Bandodkar, the merger issue intensified, despite expressions of alarm by the Government of India that too rapid a move towards merger would adversely affect the position of minority groups opposed to union with a neighbouring state. Although it claimed to be an integrating agent, by promoting regional as opposed to national integration, the MG's campaigns for merger with Maharashtra, in fact, exacerbated sectarian differences.

The individual who led the campaign for merger was Dayand Bandodkar, who simultaneously served as chief minister and president of the Maharashtrawadi Gomantak Party. 'When he entered politics Bandodkar was anything but a politician or one interested in public affairs' (Esteves 1971: 150). A merchant who had become wealthy because of mining ventures, Bandodkar acquired a reputation among the masses as a sportsman and a philanthropist. Always reiterating that he was a loyal Congressman, Bandodkar—like many other prominent non-Brahman Goans—broke ranks with the party over the merger issue. Originally regarded as the MG's financier, he did not even contest the 1963 elections. When no individual emerged as a potential chief minister from the MG candidates that were elected by the voters, he was literally drafted for the job by the Maharashtra Praja Socialist leader Nath Pai.[12] Elected to the Assembly in a by-election, Bandodkar was initially perceived as being a caretaker chief minister until merger was achieved.

Since it regarded its victory as an endorsement of merger with Maharashtra, the MGP carried out a series of measures designed to promote that end. The Bandodkar administration promoted Marathi as the language of government and education, while denigrating Konkani. It passed a resolution in the Goa Assembly demanding the merger of Goa with Maharashtra and Daman and Diu with Gujarat,[13] and enacted tenancy legislation which gave property to those who worked the land at the expense of those Goans—mainly Christians—who lived abroad or worked in Bombay but maintained land in the territory. Perhaps most offensive, the government inundated the bureaucracy at all levels with 1,100 deputized civil servants from Maharashtra at a time when qualified Goans were available to fill the positions (Carvalho 1966: 6). As a majority of the deputationists were from Maharashtra, the impression was that their primary function was to promote merger, not administer the territory.

The communalist tactics of Bandodkar[14] provoked intense resistance and succeeded in uniting the Catholic and Brahman communities that were opposed to merger. The opposition response to these measures was twofold: the United Goans staged walkouts from the Assembly and a non-party Council of Direct Action was formed to stage extra-parliamentary agitations such as *satyagrahas*, marches, and *hartals*. By August 1966 these activities were seriously disrupting the economy of the territory.

The Government of India was concerned with the escalation in the number of communal demonstrations and the rhetoric that accompanied them. Some MG leaders went so far as to state that the people who had opposed Goa's liberation were now opposing Goa's merger.[15] At various times Bandodkar claimed his opponents had 'anti-nationalist attitudes' or were 'supported by foreign interests.'[16] Bandodkar, in turn, was called 'a rank communalist and casteist' by Ravindra Kelekar, who headed the Council for Direct Action.[17]

With Congress-dominated legislatures in Maharashtra unanimously supporting merger and Mysore endorsing the status quo, opposition parties in those states, particularly the Praja Socialist, Communist, and Jan Sangh, were capitalizing—as they did prior to liberation—on the ruling party's dilemma in Goa. As a way out of the predicament, the Congress parliamentary board on September 3, 1966 recommended that the Government of India conduct an opinion poll—the only plebiscite in the country's history—to ascertain the preferences of the people of Goa, Daman and Diu. The issue to be decided before the scheduled February Assembly elections was whether people in the former Portuguese possessions wished to retain the union territory status or be merged with a neighbouring state. The electorate in Goa would decide if they wished to be merged with Maharashtra, and voters in Daman and Diu would indicate if they wanted a merger with Gujarat. While the anti-mergerists were hampered by the fact that Goans resident elsewhere in the country were denied the right to vote in the poll, they profited from the fact that alternatives did not include statehood, since three choices would have split the anti-merger camp. The new prime minister, Mrs Indira Gandhi's decision that Goans should have the right to self-determination within the Indian Union was consistent with the dictates of both her predecessors (see 'Goa and India' 1965). When the bill passed Parliament after a heated debate in December, the Bandodkar government resigned and the territory was placed under President's rule.

The contest that transpired during the one month interval between the imposition of central administration and the January 17, 1967

Opinion Poll, by all accounts witnessed the most unprecedented and intense political activity in Goa's history, including a house to house enrollment of new voters that resulted in 25,796 people being added to the electoral rolls (Esteves 1986: 128). The campaign was equally intense. There were 1,200 meetings and 800 processions during the 32 day campaign—an average of 30 meetings and 15 processions per day (ibid.: 136). The activity elicited a turnout of nearly eighty-two per cent of the voters—compared with seventy-five per cent in Goa proper (excluding Daman and Diu) in 1963. Significantly, the turnout was 87.43 per cent in the Old Conquests and 82.93 per cent in the New Conquests. Turnout exceeded ninety per cent in nine of the territory's twenty-eight constituencies; thirteen more polled over eighty per cent; and was over seventy per cent in the remaining six.

The results rejected the contention that integration with India would be achieved only by merger with Maharashtra and Gujarat. With their identity at stake, the Goans rejected merger by a vote of 172,191 to 138,170—a substantial majority of 34,021 out of 317,633 votes cast. The fact that 60,000 more Hindus than Catholics voted indicates that there was a significant crossover of non-Christians in all parts of the territory. Anti-mergerists made significant gains over their 1963 performance in virtually every constituency. Their 'two leaves' symbol garnered 54.20 per cent compared to 43.50 per cent for the pro-mergerists' 'flower.' Daman and Diu resisted merger with Gujarat, a state noted for its curbs on the consumption of alcoholic beverages, even more decisively (see Table 4.2).

Similarly, within Goa there was a significant defection of MGP supporters among the toddy-tappers who believed their livelihood

Table 4.2
Results of the 1967 Opinion Poll

Region	Votes Polled	Merger	Percentage	Union Territory	Percentage
Goa*	317,633	138,170	43.50	172,191	43.50
Daman	9,671	1,149	11.89	8,254	85.34
Diu	5,948	246	4.13	5,478	92.00

Source: 'Results of the Opinion Poll Held on 16–1–67,' *Government Gazette*, No. 42 (Supplement No. 1) Series II, January 21, 1967 and No. 42 (Supplement No. 1) Series II, January 31, 1967.
* For a detailed constituency-wise breakdown see the appendix.

would be jeopardized by merger with Maharashtra. Just as the Congress had suffered from the importation of outsiders in the 1963 elections, the pro-merger forces were hurt by the intervention of Maharashtrian politicians, government employees and motor vehicles in the campaign. Despite assurances by Chief Minister V.P. Naik of Maharashtra that Goa would be given special attention in terms of economic development after merger, anti-mergerists could point to the relative backwardness of the Konkan regions in his own state as well as the advantages of having Panjim rather than Bombay serve as the administrative capital and judicial centre for the area. Moreover, since each Goan legislator was elected by an average of only 10,000 to 11,000 voters compared to an average of 150,000 in Maharashtra, Goan representation would obviously have been diluted by merger. However, the most salient explanation for the rejection of merger can be found in the alliance of the Hindu Brahmans with virtually the entire Catholic community, which had divided their vote between the Congress and the United Goans in 1963. (This is demonstrated by Amonkar et al. n.d.) In supporting autonomy for Goa, the Brahmans, who had been in the forefront of the anti-Portuguese struggle, acted out of a fear of losing their pre-eminent positions in trade and industry as well as their political leadership in the event of incorporation with Maharashtra, while the non-Brahman Hindus sought upward mobility by promoting merger.

Whereas the 1963 election campaign had highlighted sectarian differences among Goans, the 1967 Opinion Poll served to solidify Goan identity. The Opinion Poll forced those Catholics, who had gravitated to the United Goans Party in an attempt to prevent the diminution of their community's distinct culture, to cooperate with the nationalist Hindu Brahmans who traditionally supported the Congress. Following the failure of the merger campaign, it once again became permissible for Hindu Goans to emphasize their local identity by voting for the regional party and against the Congress.

The 1967 and 1972 Elections

Although the alliance between Christians and Hindu Brahmans succeeded in blocking the attempted merger with Maharashtra in

January 1967, it was unable to form a coalition that could gain control of the territory's political apparatus in the ensuing March Assembly elections. As Donald Horowitz (1985: 318) suggests, 'Once ethnic politics begins in earnest, each party, recognizing that it cannot count on defections from the other group, has the incentive to solidify the support of its own group.' In such a polarized situation, 'ethnic votes tend to drive out nonethnic votes' (ibid.: 323). Floating voters tend to have nowhere to go in a bifurcated party system and often refrain from exercising their franchise. Hence the turnout in 1967 dropped to 65.71 per cent from its 1963 level of 70.45 per cent. When seat adjustments between the Congress and United Goans failed to materialize, the Bandodkar government returned to power as the MGP kept its 16–12 margin in the Assembly. The MG retained its forty per cent share of the popular vote, while the UG, without the competition of the Congress, attracted nearly thirty-eight per cent (Table 4.3).

Table 4.3
Results of the 1967 Assembly Elections

Party	Candidates	Valid Votes	Percentage	Seats
MG	25	110,991	40.37	16
UG	30	104,426	37.98	12
Others	171	59,504	21.65	2
Total	226	274,921 out of 418,404	65.71	30

Source: *Assembly Elections Ready Reference 1994: 28.*

As the Congress did not compete formally, the results suggest Hindu Brahman voters were not prepared to support a communal party like the United Goans. It was their view that, 'The UGP advocated Konkani and Statehood precisely to cover its communal intentions.'[18] Hence, despite fielding sixteen of twenty-six candidates from the majority community in the 1967 elections and having Hindus serve in organizational offices, the United Goans were never able to convince voters that they represented all segments of the populace. Similarly, even though the MGP included Brahmans such as Vasant Joshi in their electoral lists and appointed Catholics like Anthony D'Souza[19] to the cabinet, such gestures were regarded by most Goans as a facade designed to legitimate the party's pretense of possessing a secular character. As Horowitz (1985: 320) suggests, communal parties can engage in such tactics, precisely because their core voters will support the party identified with their own ethnic group, no matter who the individual candidates in any constituency happen to be.

When the Congress and United Goans came to an agreement to support each other's parliamentary candidates in 1971, the Congress won the North and the UG retained the South seat it had captured in 1967. Although it was maintained by some that Goa had entered the mainstream of Indian politics (Saksena 1974), the results of the 1972 elections indicate otherwise. In that year the Congress once more fielded a full slate of candidates, while it again won only Daman at a time Mrs Gandhi's supporters were sweeping the rest of the country (Table 4.4). Despite several personal appearances by Prime Minister Indira Gandhi in Goa, the effect of her efforts was to mandate a 18–10 MGP margin over the UGP. The Congress won less than fourteen per cent of the popular vote, compared to nearly thirty-eight per cent for the MG and 32 per cent for the UG (see Esteves 1972). Clearly the MGP was kept in office not by its own achievements but by a divided opposition.

Table 4.4
Results of the 1972 Assembly Elections

Party	Candidates	Valid Votes	Percentage	Seats
MG	23	112,860	37.52	18
UG	26	96,184	31.97	10
INC	19	41,032	13.97	1
Others	70	50,746	16.87	1
Totals	138	300,822 out of 451,484 eligible	66.63	30

Source: *Assembly Elections Ready Reference 1994: 30–31.*

Pre-Institutional Politics

While hardly cohesive entities, parties that draw their support on an ascriptive basis act as the organizational expression of the communities they represent. Yet, as Horowitz (1985: 348) suggests, the main feature of a polarized ethnic party system is the fact that it produces stable parties but unstable politics. While both the MG and UG engaged in flirtations with various national parties and endured numerous splits, their leaders were unwilling to surrender local independence and become subservient to organizations based in New Delhi. This reality was attributable to the communal nature of their support and the personal nature of their organizations.

Both the MGP[20] and the UGP were more like personal extensions of the Bandodkar and Sequeira families than institutionalized political party organizations in the textbook sense. In testimony presented at a 1972 trial, Erasmo de Sequeira, member of parliament for South Goa, and son of United Goans Party president and leader of the opposition in the Legislative Assembly Dr Jack Sequeira, revealed that based on knowledge he had as general secretary of the United Goans, that party had held no elections to its working committee since its founding, had no office premises, and kept no records.[21] In the face of repeated charges of autocratic rule by their leadership, both parties suffered a series of factional splits that paved the way for the intrusion of national political parties.

The Maharashtrawadi Gomantak Party

The political history of Goa during its first ten years of democratic politics should be seen as not only the struggle of non-Brahmans against the higher caste Hindus and Catholics, but also as Bandodkar's attempt to dominate the Maharashtrawadi Gomantak Party. Hence, despite the fact that it won the largest number of seats in the 1963, 1967, 1972, and 1977 Assembly elections and had governed the territory for nearly sixteen years, the MGP should not be seen as having provided a stable administration. The party, almost from its beginnings, suffered from disintegrative tendencies. Even before the first elections some of the founding members, including J.J. Shinkre, who was later a member of parliament, accused Bandodkar of handing control of the party to outsiders. Other elements associated with P.P. Shirodkar, the first speaker of the Goa Assembly, demanded that Bandodkar resign in 1964 because he had failed to fulfil the party's promise to bring about merger with Maharashtra within six months. Those on the left of the party, such as its initial vice president M.N. Lawande, became disenchanted over the government's lack of progressive economic policies, and claimed that after 1967 Bandodkar had sold out to the mine owners.[22]

By far the most common complaint against Bandodkar's leadership was that it was dictatorial. Any independent sources of strength within the party were suppressed. When long-time Bandodkar ally and general secretary of the party M.S. Prabhu was deemed too powerful, he was attacked by the chief minister in the press[23] and forced out of his position. Professor Gopal Mayekar, minister of education and tourism, was humiliatingly relieved of his tourism portfolio while attending a meeting of state ministers on that subject.

As a result of these actions and Bandodkar's insistence on holding both the party presidency and chief ministership, seven MLAs, including two cabinet ministers (Anthony D'Souza and Mayekar) and Deputy Speaker Monju Gaoankar, withdrew their support from the government in 1970 and demanded that K.B. Naik be installed as party president. As the Assembly was not in session, President's rule was not imposed by Delhi. Before the Naik group, composed of hard-line pro-merger forces, could ally with the Sequeira group that championed statehood in a strange marriage of convenience, they were outmanoeuvred by Bandodkar, who enticed five United Goan MLAs to his side. When the Assembly reconvened in August, Bandodkar was thus able to win a vote of confidence and maintain himself in power until the 1972 elections. At that time Bandodkar scored his biggest victory, capturing eighteen seats. The magnitude of that success was probably enhanced by the fact that the Naik rebels, who formed a New Maharashtrawadi Gomantak Party, garnered almost five per cent of the votes and fragmented the anti-MGP vote (see Table 4.4).

Despite his deficiencies as an administrator, Bandodkar had become a skillful politician, adept at mobilizing the non-Brahman masses against the so-called 'vested interests' at election time or blaming New Delhi for any alleged administrative shortcomings in the union territory. Nevertheless, he was careful to maintain working relationships with his fellow mine owners who dominate the economy and control the press in Goa. His personal ties to Maharashtra politicians from all parties assured that he would have friends in New Delhi no matter who was in power there. As Aurliano Fernandes (1997: 14) suggests, Bandodkar is the only Goan politician to have a mass base. All other chief ministers have been merely leaders of their legislative parties. After a decade in office Bandodkar had become a political institution, as he had managed to convert both the Government of Goa and the MGP into his personal fiefdoms. Hence, upon Bandodkar's death in August 1973, he was succeeded by his daughter Mrs Shashikala Kakodkar as president of the MGP and chief minister, even though she was only a junior minister at the time.

The Emergence of National Politics

The communal pattern of politics in Goa prevented the Indian National Congress from playing the key electoral and integrative role that it did elsewhere in post-colonial India. Instead, national identity in Goa was advanced by non-Brahman Hindu castes that sought incorporation into the neighbouring state of Maharashtra, and a Christian minority that sought to protect its identity through statehood within the larger Indian Union. Although both communities claimed to be promoting national integration, their tactics exacerbated local cleavages. Before the Congress could play an effective role in the affairs of the region, the communal pattern of politics had to be broken and the local party unit had to be legitimated by local talent. This occurred during the period of Mrs Gandhi's imposition of internal Emergency in the mid-1970's when the mainly Catholic United Goans joined non-Brahman Hindu defectors from the MGP in the Congress. However, the Congress which emerged triumphant in the 1980 elections may be seen more as a holding company of the opposition in Goa than as an extension of a national organization. Its victory in the 1980 elections and subsequent amalgamation with Mrs Gandhi's organization accelerated Goa's national integration and culminated in statehood.

The Break up of the United Goans

Just like their MGP adversaries, the United Goans also suffered a series of splits—some of which were based upon the alleged domination of the party by Christian Brahmans. In late 1966, eight of the twelve UG MLAs under the leadership of Dr Alvaro de Loyola Furtado left the party to protest against their leader Dr Jack Sequeira's failure to press for a clear-cut referendum choice between statehood and merger, and what they believed was his flirtation with the Indian National Congress.[24] The Sequeira group, which continued to dominate the Catholic vote by its possession of the 'hand' electoral symbol associated with St Francis Xavier, survived this split and another one in 1970, but fell apart irreparably in 1974. Its demise was exacerbated when the Coca Cola plant operated by the Sequeira family became involved in a bloody labour dispute.

The third and final split in the UG was precipitated by Erasmo de Sequeira's decision to join Charan Singh's Bhartiya Lok Dal (BLD) group in Parliament. Sequeira's action was a product of the national perspective he had acquired as a representative in Delhi for several years,[25] but it also reflected the party's deterioration as a force in Goan politics. The decision of the Congress to contest the 1972 elections had caused a decline in UG fortunes.[26] By 1974 even the party's Catholic bastions were no longer safe, as the MG came so close to capturing the Benaulim seat in a by-election that the matter had to be settled in court. While the bulk of the United Goans moved into the Indian National Congress during the Emergency in 1976, the Sequeira group later joined the Janata coalition. By 1977 national political parties finally emerged in Goa, although it was more accurately a situation where local factions adopted all-India labels.

The Attainment of Legitimacy by the Congress Party

The intrusion of national politics into Goa was reinforced by the decision of Pratapsingh Rane, law minister in the MGP government, to join the Congress party without resigning from the cabinet before the 1977 elections. Rane, a Texas-educated admirer of President John F. Kennedy,[27] was from a prominent land-owning family. He had attended school in Poona in Maharashtra and worked in the industrial city of Jamshedpur in Bihar. Like many others who were opposed to the merger with Maharashtra, Rane had entered politics at the invitation of Bandodkar, but found that he could not work with the late chief minister's daughter. Related by marriage to officials in the Congress government of the neighbouring state of Karnataka and by blood to prominent princely families like the Scindias in north India, Rane had a national view of politics. His entry as a prominent non-Brahman Hindu gave the local Congress Party credibility as a secular institution. Significantly, Rane's re-election on the Congress ticket from the remote Satari constituency, a traditional MGP stronghold, marked the first time that someone who had abandoned that party had been returned to the Assembly.

The 1977 Elections

While politics in Goa were changing, the MGP, despite its initial courting of Catholic voters in the 1974 Benaulim by-election, failed to adjust. Whereas her father had offered tickets to prominent Goans regardless of their community, Mrs Kakodkar, in an attempt to solidify her own position, narrowed the party's base and in the process antagonized not only the Catholic minority, but other groups as well. Although her caste group constituted a minute fraction of the Hindu community, a disproportionate share of the party's 1977 candidates were drawn from it. Moreover, she literally wrote off constituencies that were vital to the party's continued control of the legislature. She made no appearances in the north Goa Pale constituency of A.K.S. Usgaonkar, who had been her father's senior minister and a potential rival as his successor in 1973.[28] She refused to ask Baban Naik, who held the prestigious Panjim constituency to run for re-election.[29] Both seats were lost by the MGP.

As a result of an ineffective campaign, the total number of seats captured by the MGP dropped to fifteen. Although its electoral percentage held at over thirty-eight per cent, the support of independent members from Diu and Daman, who were named speaker and deputy speaker, was required to form the new MGP government. Only the nearly even distribution of the opposition vote caused by the emergence of the Janata Party in the June Assembly races prevented the rout of the MGP. The Janata won nearly twenty-three per cent of the popular vote, and the Congress garnered almost twenty-nine per cent. The Janata had not been a factor in the March parliamentary elections, as both its candidates, including Erasmo de Sequeira the two-term incumbent from South Goa, were badly defeated. However, the Assembly contest occurred at the time many Bombay Goans traditionally visit their family homesteads, and their influence is believed to have been a factor in the Bardez results in north Goa. In addition, many Janata Party notables, including George Fernandes, addressed election rallies on behalf of local candidates. While the Janata picked up only

three seats for its efforts compared to ten for the Congress, the
electoral competition of these two parties made possible MG
pluralities for the first time in the predominantly Catholic constituencies of Calangute, Tivim, and Dabolim and ensured narrow
wins in its traditional seats of Cumbarjua and Ponda. Ironically,
because of the splinter factor, the intrusion of national politics
initially benefited the Maharashtrawadi Gomantak Party (see Table
4.5).

Table 4.5
Results of the 1977 Assembly Elections

Party	Candidates	Valid Votes	Percentage	Seats
MG	29	116,339	38.61	15
Congress	28	86,561	28.73	10
Janata	30	69,122	22.94	3
Others	58	29,315	9.73	1
Total	145	301,337 out of 485,811 eligible	62.03	30

Source: *Assembly Elections Ready Reference 1994: 32–33.*

The Fall of the MG Government

The 1977 campaign continued after the results were known. A
body called the Peoples' Democratic Front, with ties to parties and
interest groups across the political spectrum, was formed to organize public demonstrations in an attempt to bring down the Kakodkar
government. In a situation where the governing party did not have
an absolute majority in a thirty-member legislature, the prospects
for instability were manifest. The selection of the cabinet nearly
caused the government to fall. The traditional manner of MG
cabinet selection—a Bandodkar as chief minister, and the inclusion
of one Brahman, one Christian, plus an additional middle caste
Hindu—was no longer workable. Other MLAs refused to be satisfied with appointment to potentially lucrative posts, such as membership on the boards of banks, consumer cooperatives, or the
State Transport Authority. Younger, better educated Hindu back-
benchers were disenchanted when they were passed over for inclusion in an undistinguished council of ministers, and some of those

who were included were resentful that Mrs Kakodkar retained three-quarters of the portfolios for herself (Fernandes 1997: 55). Those members of the Assembly who were elected from traditional non-MGP seats demanded special consideration, so that they might be returned in future contests. Instead of accommodating them, Mrs Kakodkar's response was to engage in vituperative public exchanges—a tactic that jeopardized the very existence of her government. Her fragile majority was repeatedly saved by the tie-breaking votes of Speaker Narayan Fugro.

Mrs Kakodkar's government survived for two years only because a Janata government was in power in New Delhi, while the principal opposition in Goa was the Congress-S affiliated with former union minister Swaran Singh, an opponent of Indira Gandhi. This situation was compounded by a condition that further impeded coordination of the opposition: The effective legislative opposition was provided by the three-man Janata Party contingent under the leadership of Madhav Bir, while the Congress group of ten by comparison was ineffectual. With respect to the organizational wings of the two parties, the situation was reversed. Appointed from Delhi on the basis of their loyalty to Prime Minister Morarji Desai, none of the individuals who controlled the Janata Party in Goa had ever won territorial office. The Janata Party thus replicated the historic Congress model for failure in Goa.

The Kakodkar government finally found itself in a minority position during the budget session of April 1979 when Law Minister Shankar Laad, who resented the chief minister's interference with his portfolios, withdrew his support. Although her government had been defeated in the Assembly, Mrs Kakodkar refused to resign. The centre, unwilling to allow a cabinet of MG defectors to govern with Congress-S support, imposed President's rule on April 28. The unruly character of Mrs Kakodkar's supporters in the Assembly after they lost their majority served to discredit the MG in the forthcoming election. The lack of grace with which the Kakodkar government fell proved to be a significant liability during the ensuing campaign. In retrospect, Mrs Kakodkar's decision not to let a coalition cabinet composed of MGP defectors take office with the support of the local Janata and Congress parties proved to be a serious error. Given the conflicting ambitions and contradictory goals of its components, such an arrangement would have had a difficult time persisting. Had she followed the example of Mrs

Gandhi and gone into opposition, Mrs Kakodkar would have been in a position to attack the record of her opponents. Instead, she began the 1979–80 election campaign on the defensive.

Seldom had a politician's fall from grace been so dramatic. When she assumed office at the age of thirty-eight following the sudden death of her father in August 1973, Mrs Kakodkar had the support of most Goans. Her initial efforts to bring the Catholic voters of Salcette into the MGP fold nearly proved successful. Yet, within a few short years she had managed to squander this reservoir of good will. She showed indifference to strikes for higher fares by bus owners that inconvenienced commuters and disrupted the economy of the territory. Her response to violent protests by the traditional fishermen against encroachments by the mechanized trawlers had been to blame the Catholic Church for promoting the agitation. In addition to rekindling communal tensions, she failed to alleviate the growing unemployment that followed the expansion of education during the decade of the 1970s. Instead of addressing charges of corruption and maladministration, Mrs Kakodkar dismissed them as political attacks. Rather than broadening her base in an attempt to adjust to change, she refused to democratize the party and relied more heavily on her husband, a tactic which proved to be a considerable liability.[30]

Discontent within the MGP was widespread. Amrut Kansar, the party's sitting MP from the North Goa constituency, had become disillusioned with the territorial government's failure to prevent the powerful mining industry from damaging agricultural land.[31] He broke with Mrs Kakodkar and lent his support to the dissenters. Unlike her father, Mrs Kakodkar was remote from party workers. Intra-party communications were practically nonexistent, as even back-benchers in the Assembly were kept in the dark about political matters.[32] There was considerable resentment at the way the Kakodkar family monopolized all aspects of both party and governmental affairs, including the distribution of electoral tickets and cabinet portfolios. The chief minister's retention of seventy-five per cent of the portfolios and her interference in the other twenty-five per cent contributed to the decision of both Mr Rane and Mr Laad to leave the party. The party organization was in such a state of neglect that it lacked even a register of members or a duly elected executive.[33] Members were even denied access to the rules of the party as set forth in the constitution.

Its 1963 constitution exposed the party as ideologically barren. By 1979 a political party dedicated to achieve the integration of Goa into Maharashtra, when most voters were demanding statehood, was clearly an anachronism. Promoting the Marathi language at the expense of Konkani was also counterproductive. Very few attractive candidates were willing to seek election on such an obsolete platform. Yet, if the party reneged on its commitment to merger or changed its name to the Gomantak Party, it might lose its symbol or alienate enough of its diehard supporters to suffer at the polls.

Mrs Kakodkar suffered other dilemmas. If she democratized the party, she would lose control of the apparatus. Yet, if she ticketed 'yes-men', she would be out of power, as they were unlikely to be returned to the Assembly by an increasingly sophisticated electorate. Under the circumstances, Mrs Kakodkar's strategy was to purge the party of dissidents, invite others who had left previously back into the fold, and resurrect the image of her father in MGP campaign literature—a tactic that had less utility with each successive election. While the Congress skillfully allocated tickets to numerically significant subcastes—many of which had been ignored in previous MG cabinets—Mrs Kakodkar's own *jati* (sub-caste) the Gomantak Maratha Samaj, was disproportionately represented in her party's election list. Thus the MG's traditional assertion that it alone represented the *bahujan samaj*, or lower caste masses, had a hollow ring in the 1980 elections. The disparities in the standard of living meant that the *bahujan samaj*, or non-Brahman Hindu masses no longer constituted one political force. While the MGP with its emphasis on regionalism as opposed to economic development had become obsolete, the Congress had refined the art of sectarianism to a new level. Despite its stated emphasis on modernity, the Congress with its skillful ticketing of demographically significant *jatis* in crucial constituencies, perfected the art of traditional politics in Goa. It had its choice of aspirants. While in the past the exodus had been to the MG ticket list, in 1979 potential Lok Dal and Janata candidates deserted those lines for places on the Congress list.

The 1979–80 Campaign

Although territorial elections had been initially scheduled for October 1979, they were later combined with the national poll on

January 3, 1980. Since all party platforms, including the MG, advanced statehood, promoted the Konkani language, and agreed on most other points, the parties lacked the communal distinctiveness that had been evident in previous contests. This lack of party distinctiveness was reflected in the final list of candidates. Eighteen out of the thirty candidates on the MG list formerly belonged to the Congress, while twelve Congress-U nominees affiliated with neighbouring Karnataka Chief Minister Devraj Urs who had broken with Mrs Gandhi, were formerly members of the MGP (A. Rubinoff 1980).

While not having the instruments of power at its disposal was a disadvantage for the MGP, that was counterbalanced by opportunities that were presented by the collapse of the Janata government in Delhi. The deteriorating situation at the centre enabled the MGP to argue that Goa would be better off with regional party rule in Panjim.

Despite the role its legislative contingent had played in leading the attack on the Kakodkar government in the Assembly, the Janata Party was in the weakest condition prior to the election. The disintegration of the Janata, always a top-down entity, was replicated in Goa. The Erasmo Sequeira–Pandurang Shirodkar group, first claimed to be the 'lawful organ of the Janata Party,'[34] then threatened to form a new local party, and finally followed Charan Singh into the Lok Dal. Sequeira, former member of parliament for South Goa, after a two-year absence from politics, organized a civil disobedience campaign that protested the imposition of President's rule. The movement's abysmal failure was a portent of things to come for the Janata-S group. The fact that the Lok Dal–Congress-U alliance at the centre was not duplicated in Goa was a reflection of how unnecessary it was for the Congress-U to accommodate the once influential Sequeira family. Ultimately, because each had so little to offer the other parties and as they were rivals in Delhi, the Lok Dal and Janata were forced to go it alone in Goa. Already burdened with Prime Minister Desai's identification with the imposition of prohibition, a ban on cow slaughter and freedom of religion legislation designed to discourage conversions, the Janata Party was now held responsible for the imposition of President's rule. Having alienated the Catholic voters they had courted only three years before, the Janata Party was now discredited in the 1980 elections.

The main imponderable in the campaign was how much a factor the Congress-I constituted. While most of the undivided party had followed Dr Wilfred de Souza into the Congress-S camp after the split of January 1978 and then adopted the Congress-U banner of neighbouring Karnataka Chief Minister Devraj Urs, a handful of loyalists like Purshottam Kakodkar formed the Congress-I in Goa. Although it was an organization that existed primarily on paper, the party's main trump card was not Indira Gandhi—despite her recognized popularity among Catholics in Goa—but the party's national 'hand' election symbol. Congress-U leaders were concerned that unless the Congress-I was accommodated, former United Goan voters in the south *taluka* of Salcette would divide the Catholic vote, causing a repetition of the 1977 Bardez situation that had enabled the MG to win pluralities in normally Christian strongholds. The opportunity for an arrangement came when Mrs Gandhi, as part of her campaign tour, addressed a rally in Panjim on December 13. Under the terms of an agreement that was struck, Purshottam Kakodkar was to be endorsed for the North parliamentary seat along with six Congress-I candidates in northern districts. In return, the Congress-I would not oppose Congress-U candidates in the remaining constituencies. Predictably, the pact broke down when several of the originally designated Congress-U candidates ran as independents and advertised their connection with Dr de Souza. Two who did so, Vishnu Naik in Panjim and Chandrakant Chodankar, won election.

Thus, with the exception of Bicholim where all parties endorsed Harish Zantye against Mrs Kakodkar and Diu where Speaker Narayan Fugro had similar backing against its candidate, the MG faced a divided opposition in multicornered contests. This familiar pattern led *The Times of India* to predict that the 'MGP was all set to emerge as the single largest party' in Goa,[35] but unlike the situation in past contests, every party but the Congress-U was so weak as to be insignificant.

Not subject to significant inroads by Janata, as had been the case three years previously, the Congress-U won a victory of landslide proportions capturing nineteen of the thirty Assembly seats. The Congress obliterated the MGP, reducing it to just seven seats and defeating the former chief minister in two constituencies. The Congress out-polled the MG for the first time, while the Janata and Lok Dal could respectively muster only around 4 per cent and 1.72 per cent of the votes (See Table 4.6).

Table 4.6
Results of the 1980 Assembly Elections

Party	Candidates	Valid Votes	Percentage	Seats
MG	30	121,714	35.39	7
Congress	28	142,589	41.38	19
Janata	23	14,431	4.19	0
Others	96	66,117	19.17	4
Total	177	344,851 out of 522,652 eligible	65.99	30

Source: *Assembly Elections Ready Reference 1994: 34–35.*

The results, as *The Times of India*[36] pointed out, marked the initial time that Goa had voted for a national party—but in supporting the Congress-U which did poorly everywhere else, the union territory had reasserted its insularity: No Congress-I candidate was successful in Goa, despite the trend elsewhere in India.

Interestingly, several former MGP MLAs, including Vassu Gaonkar in Canacona, and two MG rebels, Dilkush Desai in Rivona and Dayanand Narvekar in Tivim were returned on the Congress-U ticket. Another MGP rebel Chandrakant Chodankar, who many believe precipitated the 1979 crisis in the party, was returned as an independent with Congress-U support from Siolim. Aside from the defeat of Speaker Narayan Fugro in Diu—a special target of the MGP—the only major victory for that party was in the Northern parliamentary constituency where Mrs Samogeeta Rane, a relative of Pratapsingh Rane, was elected to Parliament. With respect to the Assembly races, only a massive increase in votes in the two remote non-contiguous constituencies in Daman and Diu kept the total MG vote respectable. In numerical terms it actually increased from 116,339 in 1977 to 121,714 in 1980. However, because the electorate had increased from 485,111 to 522,652, its percentage of the total declined by nearly two percentage points. By itself the Congress-U polled 134,651 or 38.51 per cent, an increase from 86,561 and 28.73 per cent in 1977. If one combines the total Congress vote, it reaches 41.87 per cent. Even though this figure is larger if one includes the totals of the Congress-U-backed independents, it is clear that the key variable in the election was the drop in the Janata vote from almost twenty-three per cent in 1977 to just over four per cent in 1980. Since the combined Janata–

Congress total in 1977 exceeded fifty-one per cent, it is clear that the MGP was living on borrowed time. Hence, despite the reality that it won the largest number of seats on four occasions, one could say that the Maharashtrawadi Gomantak Party never won Assembly elections in Goa. Rather a divided opposition lost them.

In reality, there was little the MGP could have done to stem the Congress onslaught. Mathematically it faced an impossible task in 1980. For one thing, three of its fifteen 1977 victories, those in Tivim, Dabolim and Calangute, had been attributable to the Janata wave. While it won Pale, owing to a plurality made possible by the candidacy of a Congress MLA who did not receive renomination, and secured Daman and Diu for the first time, so deep was the electorate's disenchantment with the Goa's traditional ruling party that the traditional MG seats of Mapusa, Ponda, Siroda, Sanguem, Canacona, Rivona and Bicholim were lost.

The defeat of the MGP in 1980 marked the emergence of non-communal issue-oriented politics in Goa, for the voters exercised their franchise on the basis of governmental performance for the first time. In the terminology of the Rudolphs (1967: 26), politics had evolved from horizontal to differential mobilization as political parties became able to make appeals based on ideology, sentiment and interest. However, it is difficult to tell if the Congress' victory formula represented a movement towards modern or a refinement of traditional politics. On the one hand, the Congress made an appeal to the growing number of voters who profited from education in the two decades since liberation. On the other hand, it expertly allocated tickets to numerically significant subcastes—many of which had been ignored in previous MG cabinets.

In any event, the twenty-three seats the Congress and its allies won in 1980 proved to be an embarrassment of riches. As was the case elsewhere in India, political conflict in Goa began to be expressed within the Congress instead of between parties. Shortly after the results were tabulated, Eduardo Faleiro, the Congress-U MP for South Goa, crossed the floor of the Lok Sabha and joined the Indira group. Mrs Kakodkar, who was defeated in her own constituency, brought five of the seven remaining MGP MLAs with her into the Congress camp. At about the same time, local units of the two Congress parties were amalgamated under Mrs Gandhi's banner, a prudent strategy since she was in power in Delhi and a union territory is heavily dependent on the centre.

Characteristically, Mrs Gandhi replaced those in the territorial party apparatus who had successfully conducted the election campaign with Nehru family loyalists, despite their record of repeated electoral failures in Goa.

As Chief Minister Pratapsingh Rane was not in the position of being both chief minister and party leader, his attempt to accommodate the various components of his majority encountered difficulties (see Fernandes 1997: 89). Consequently, there was no shortage of disappointed politicians. Almost immediately factions coalesced around two ministers, both former United Goans—A.N. Naik, a Hindu and Dr Wilfred de Souza, a Christian. Ironically, their rivalry and the chief minister's support in New Delhi at a time the union territory hosted the Commonwealth meetings in 1983 and celebrated the Exposition of St Francis in 1984, enabled Rane to survive repeated crises.

The 1984 Fragmentation

Prior to the 1984 elections the splits in the Congress coalition became manifest: de Souza and his primarily Catholic followers formed a new organization, the Goa Congress (GC); Mrs Kakodkar founded a party named after her late father; and meanwhile the MGP continued to exist as a rump force. As *Goa Today* put it, 'Never before has Goa had so many political groupings to be taken seriously.'[37] However, this fragmentation worked to the advantage of the ruling Congress party in the December 1984 poll. Mrs Kakodkar's entry garnered only about seven per cent of the votes, but reduced the MGP's share to less than twenty-two per cent—just over half of what the Congress obtained. Despite the fact that Goa Congress collected nearly seventeen per cent of the votes, the Congress increased its share of the votes to 39.41 per cent. As a result of this splintering, the INC won eighteen seats, the MGP took eight, the Goa Congress claimed one and independents—who captured a significant ten per cent of the vote—captured three (Table 4.7).

Ironically, both de Souza and Naik, as well as Mrs Kakodkar, were defeated. As one commentator put it, 'Rane continues to rule the roost, profiting more by his political opponents' constant bungling rather than through any intrinsic leadership qualities.'[38] Nevertheless, factional rivalry within the Congress and support from New Delhi enabled Rane to continue in office for a decade. His legacy would be the attainment of statehood for Goa.

Table 4.7
Results of the 1984 Assembly Elections

Party	Candidates	Valid Votes	Percentage	Seats
MG	26	86,100	21.12	8
INC	30	160,664	39.41	18
GC	28	67,349	16.52	1
BBSP	23	28,271	6.93	0
Others	135	65,323	16.02	3
Total	242	407,707 out of 586,709 eligible	69.49	30

Source: *Assembly Elections Ready Reference 1994: 36–37.*

END NOTES

1. In the case of *Rev. Mons. Sebastlaõ Xavier dos Remedios Monteiro v State*, AIR 1968 Goa, Daman and Diu 17 (v. 55 C6), a Goan born Roman Catholic priest unsuccessfully challenged the annexation. After refusing an Indian passport, he declined to register as a foreigner and demanded that he be allowed to stay in Goa as a Portuguese national.
2. *Lok Sabha Debates*, Second Series, Vol. IV, No. 44, April 14, 1961, column 11321.
3. *Rajya Sabha Debates*, Vol. L, No. 14, December 4, 1964, columns 2452–53.
4. *The Times of India* (New Delhi), March 30, 1962.
5. See 'Exit the Lotus Eaters,' *Economist*, May 5, 1962, p. 462.
6. According to one scholar, 'The idea of merger of Goa with Maharashtra was taken by the National Congress (Goa) from Dattatraya Venkatash Pai who had propounded it at a meeting in Bombay in July 1946 of the Maharashtra Ekikaran Parishad' (Esteves 1976: 479–80). According to another, the impetus for a political party to bring about merger of Goa with Maharashtra can be traced to the formation of the Azad Gomantak Dal in Belgaum in 1954 with the support of the Hindu Mahasabha and the Jan Sangh (Halappa et al. 1964: 40–41).
7. 'Article Two of the MGP Constitution.' I am grateful to Mr J.J. Shinkre, a founder of the party, for making this document available to me in Ponda on May 24, 1979.
8. This source is a useful account of the early period of territorial politics. A revised version was published by Sterling of New Delhi in 1986.
9. In reality, Mysore's intentions were more to deny Goa to Maharashtra than to absorb the territory itself.
10. *The Times of India* (New Delhi), December 13, 1963.
11. *The Hindustan Times* (New Delhi), December 14, 1963.
12. Confirmed by a number of interviews.

13. *Legislative Assembly of Goa, Daman and Diu Debates*, Vol. II., No. 5, January 22, 1965, p. 151.
14. Bandodkar claimed he was in favour of 'a Hindu' as opposed to a secular state. *Navhind Times* (Panaji), June 7, 1970.
15. Statement by Muk nd Shinkre, M.P. in the *Navhind Times*, January 18, 1965.
16. Ibid., June 15, 1966 and July 4, 1966.
17. Ibid., July 11, 1966.
18. Chandrakant Keni, 'Need for a Regional Party,' *Goa Today*, May 1995, p. 47.
19. D'Souza was married to a Hindu. Interview, Bombay, June 30, 1979.
20. MGP vice president, R. Pankar, claimed he was appointed to the post in 1970 by Bandodkar without prior knowledge or consultation. Interview, Mapusa, May 28, 1979.
21. *Navhind Times*, July 26–27, 1972.
22. Interview, Panjim, May 4, 1979.
23. *Rashtramat* (Margao), June 7, 1970.
24. Interview, Chinchinim, June 6, 1979.
25. Interview, Panjim, May 16, 1979.
26. Hector Simoes, 'The Goa Elections,' *Navhind Times*, March 29, 1972.
27. Interview, Sanquelim, May 30, 1979.
28. Interview, Panjim, June 22, 1979.
29. Interview, Panjim, May 25, 1979.
30. See the article 'Change in Goa,' *The Times of India* (New Delhi), April 25, 1979, p. 8.
31. Interview, Panjim, May 5, 1979.
32. Perhaps with good reason: It was reported in the press that five additional MLAs would have joined the MG defectors if they had known in advance of Shankar Laad's intention to leave the cabinet. *Navhind Times*, April 21, 1979. Credence for this assertion is provided by the fact that several ex-MLAs opposed the party in the 1980 elections.
33. Valmiki Faleiro, 'Why They Rebelled,' *West Coast Times* (Margao), June 3, 1979, p. 3.
34. *The Times of India* (New Delhi), May 3, 1979, p. 1.
35. Ibid., January 1, 1980, p. 14.
36. Ibid., January 10, 1980, p. 6.
37. *Goa Today*, June 1984, p. 9.
38. Devika Sequeira, 'Victor by Default,' *Goa Today*, February 1987, p. 16.

Chapter 5

The Campaign for Statehood

◆

If the coming to power of a national political party in Goa was an indication of the territory's integration, its delay in becoming a full-fledged state was considered by some Goans to be a measure of their lack of integration. Union territory status was in many circles regarded as synonymous with second class citizenship. After merger with a neighbouring state as a means of securing first class status had been rejected, Goans considered union territory status to be an intermediate phase. They felt the logical progression was statehood—a status that would be a confirmation of their integration. Indeed, all major parties had endorsed such a proposal in the last three territorial elections held in 1972, 1977 and 1980.

The reasons for the delay in achieving statehood were primarily historical and political. The draft constitution of 1948 did not mention the Portuguese pockets existing as separate units in terms of an independent India (Sharma 1968: 37). The status of Goa, Daman and Diu, after their incorporation into the Indian Union, was defined by the Government of Union Territories Act of 1963, which was later amended to enhance the power of union territories in the category of Goa. Although the powers of a union territory are similar to those of a state, there are several significant differences, particularly with regard to financial matters. Since a union territory receives a 100 per cent grant from the centre, New Delhi can control its economic direction. Furthermore, a territory's ability to borrow is constrained. In addition, a union territory has no personality in the courts. The union government acts in the name of the territory which is under the administration of the Home Ministry in New Delhi; a territory's chief administrative officer is a lieutenant governor while that of a state is a governor, and at his behest or that of Parliament, the centre's capacity to intervene or delay legislation is considerable. The centre's ability to review actions taken by territorial governments can result in delays in the administration of public service, a situation that can contribute to a feeling of remoteness. In the case of Goa, its judicial system was ultimately under the jurisdiction of the High Court of Bombay.

In addition to these administrative limitations, there were political disadvantages to being a union territory as opposed to a state. Goa's representative in the Rajya Sabha was chosen by nomination and not by election in the Assembly. However, in terms of population, with two seats for just over a million people, Goa was over-represented in the Lok Sabha, compared to the rest of the country. According to the union government, Goa's small size, economic situation and lack of political stability militated against statehood (see A. Rubinoff 1992; 1995a). However, despite its relatively small numbers, Goa's population density exceeded that of the tribal states of Nagaland, Meghalaya, Manipur, and Tripura. In terms of legislative representation, states are normally required to have assemblies with a minimum of sixty delegates. This factor militated against Goa—an area the size of most state districts—as thirty seats were adequate for its geographic representation. The fact that Daman and Diu were not contiguous to Goa suggested that they would eventually be merged with Gujarat.

States are supposed to be viable economically, and this argument was applied against Goa. Former prime minister Shastri was on record as saying that in a hundred years Goa would still require economic assistance from the centre.[1] Yet, with its considerable mineral wealth and one of the best harbours in the country located at Mormugao, Goa was more viable economically than most states in the Indian Union and certainly was in a better economic position than other territories (National Council of Applied Economic Research 1970). Indeed, its government revenue rose more than fifty per cent between 1964–65 and 1975–76.[2] Budgetary deficits of union territories are subsidized to encourage development, but statehood does not preclude this possibility. While eighty-seven per cent of the revenue requirements of Nagaland are met by the union government, the need for central assistance in the case of Goa was only thirty per cent.[3] Many states such as Haryana, Nagaland, Meghalaya, Manipur, Tripura, Himachal Pradesh and

Jammu and Kashmir were more heavily subsidized on a per capita basis than Goa was as a union territory. By the same measurement, income-tax collections in Goa were consistently the second highest in the entire country. Economically, Goa did not seem deficient in terms of the requirements for statehood.

Political stability is another requisite for statehood. According to H.M. Patel, home minister in the Janata government, despite a record that included sixteen consecutive years of government by one party, Goa fell short in that respect.[4] Its record of defections, compared to most state legislatures, was not out of the ordinary; nor did it fare badly in terms of the comparative outbreak of violence. While the unstable northeastern territories were granted statehood precisely as an inducement to integration because their strategic position seemed to warrant it, Goa was denied statehood by the central government until it achieved what was regarded as a satisfactory level of emotional integration.

If this contradiction seemed like a 'catch 22' situation to average Goans, they could only blame their territorial government and themselves for not being more assertive. An MGP government whose sole purpose was to push for merger with Maharashtra was not anxious to repudiate its position. Chief Minister Bandodkar was slow to acknowledge the results of the 1967 Opinion Poll. As late as 1969 he maintained that bogus electoral rolls were responsible for the success of the anti-merger forces.[5] In September of the following year he claimed that development should precede the granting of statehood.[6] By 1971 he pronounced statehood to be his 'ultimate aim,'[7] but when the Assembly passed a United Goans Private Member's Resolution to that effect,[8] Bandodkar was absent from the House. While later that year Bandodkar endorsed 'working statehood,'[9] his daughter and successor seemed to retreat. As late as March 1976, she was on record as stating that the 'time was not right for statehood.'[10] Not until mid-October of that year did the MGP demand full-fledged statehood, and that was done by means of a non-official resolution.[11] When it became expedient for election purposes, the MG climbed on the statehood bandwagon in 1977 and 1980, but it never really pushed New Delhi on the matter.[12] While the territorial Congress publicly advocated statehood, privately its leaders recognized that the attainment of that status would deprive the party of its principal campaign issue.[13] Consequently, Goa was excluded from a major study of minority integration in India, 'unless and until [such time as] it makes increasingly greater claims on the central government for preferential treatment, greater autonomy, or both' (Schermerhorn 1978: 12).

Under the circumstances, New Delhi was slow to respond. As far as it was concerned, the union government had 'more important problems' that required its attention.[14] Both Mrs Gandhi[15] and her immediate successor Morarji Desai were on record as opposing the creation of small states. Yet in March 1972, during an election campaign, Mrs Gandhi announced that statehood would be granted to Goa at the 'appropriate time.'[16] In 1977, Railway Minister Madhu Dandavate, whose constituency in Maharashtra bordered Goa, promised the new Janata government would upgrade the union territory's status to that of a state.[17] However, his pledge was repudiated by Prime Minister Desai.[18] The return of Mrs Gandhi to office in New Delhi in 1980 and the simultaneous installation of the Congress in Panjim—the first time in history the government of Goa was of the same party as the one that controlled the centre—initially made no difference in the territory's status. However, the case of statehood for Goa could not be seen in isolation. Since any move regarding Goa was alleged to have an effect on other jurisdictions that were also demanding statehood, such as Delhi and Pondicherry, the union government proceeded cautiously.

The Language Issue

As Stanley Tambiah (1996: 22) notes, language is not merely a creative device but it also has implications for cultural identity. On account of its symbolic importance, the elevation of an ethnic group's language to a place of equality is 'the quintessential entitlement issue' (Horowitz 1985: 220). Given the linguistic basis of states in India, advocates of statehood for Goa pursued a strategy of attempting to have Konkani included in the Eighth Schedule as a recognized national language (Newman 1988). They believed that such an action would enable exams at the state level to be taken in Konkani, enhance the language's development, and expedite statehood.[19] By the same token, they believed the attainment of statehood would inevitably advance the Konkani language.

However, the Government of India was reluctant to extend the linguistic state formula to the Konkan regions as this would have required redrawing the borders of Kerala, Karnataka, and Maharashtra. Since some of these border areas were already in dispute, the so-called *Vishal Gomantak* (Greater Goa) formula had often been advanced as a way of ending these conflicts and granting Goa statehood. However, as the *Navhind Times* pointed out, merger with what are less developed and more populous parts of other states would not only create additional financial burdens for Goa, but also cause the area to lose its distinct cultural identity.[20] As Konkani has five different scripts, a separate state with a single language would not necessarily have promoted the language's development. A Greater Goa would also have diluted the influence of Goa's politicians.

While English was the language of choice for most Goans, in an attempt to exclude outsiders, Konkani became *desirable* for employment in government service.[21] The use of English in administration was a technique to avoid having to choose between Konkani and Marathi as an official language. While ninety-five per cent of Goans speak Konkani, the majority of Hindus read and write Marathi. The official language controversy was rekindled in July 1985 when the sole MLA of the communal Goa Congress Party attempted to embarrass the Rane government by moving a private member's bill making Konkani the territory's official language. Rane personally thought any measure displacing English would ensure that Goa would enter the eighteenth rather than the twentieth century, while MGP representatives who advocated Marathi referred to Konkani 'as a foreign language of the elites.'[22] Nevertheless, a few months later, the chief minister's own executive, with the backing of Eduardo Faleiro, the MP for South Goa and union minister of state for external affairs, endorsed the measure.[23]

As was the case at the time of the Opinion Poll, a coalition of Christians and Hindu Brahmans was formed to advance a political demand. This time it was the promotion of the Konkani language. The demands of the largely Christian Goa Congress were supported by the Konkani Porjecho Awaz (KPA), comprised of a handful of largely Hindu Brahman writers. This group, founded on July 29, 1986, claimed, 'The Bill is a sacred document, because for the first time in Goa's long, harsh history, it aims to give Konkani its rightful place in its homeland.'[24] In response, the All-India Congress

Committee drafted a bill making Konkani the official language, but assuring Marathi 'equal protection.' In reaction, pro-Marathi agitators set fire to government-owned vehicles and ruptured the water pipeline to Margāo, the principal city in Salcette *taluka*. The Congress was characteristically caught in the middle, unable to 'ignore the pro-Marathi lobby by pushing the official language bill nor let down Konkani protagonists by giving equal status to Marathi.'[25] Ironically, eight Congress MLAs who had defeated pro-Marathi MGP candidates in the 1984 election, now demanded a dual language formula.

The issue, clearly a device by disgruntled Congressmen to topple the Rane government, remained dormant from the July 1986 legislative session until the celebration commemorating the twenty-fifth anniversary of the liberation on December 19. Agitators claimed that 'as long as Goa remained a Union Territory and Konkani was not recognized as the official language, the Liberation was incomplete.' Alluding to developments in Assam and Mizoram, they asserted that 'the only language New Delhi understands is violence.' In the ensuing days, politicians sponsored demonstrations which attempted to create a situation whereby President's rule would be proclaimed and new elections called. 'The logic,' one commentator claimed, 'seemed to be that if the bill could not be passed without bringing down the government, the government would have to be brought down to pass the bill' (Fera 1987: 34). Accordingly, pro-Konkani demonstrators attempted to block all roads in Tiswadi and Salcette *talukas* during the height of the tourist season. Pro-Marathi agitators reacted by turning these roadblocks 'into communal traps that ensnared the agitators themselves.' In the ensuing violence, six people were killed. Fourteen companies of paramilitary troops were required to restore the peace.

In the midst of the breakdown of law and order, Prime Minister Rajiv Gandhi indicated that Goa lacked the political maturity for statehood. He implied that the language issue had to be resolved before Goa would be upgraded in status. He further indicated that the centre would not interfere in the matter which had to be decided by the territorial Assembly.[26] Nevertheless, the centre intervened to have the local Congress party's legislation passed and accepted. After the Goa Assembly adopted the Official Languages Bill which made Konkani in Devanagari script the official language and provided for the use of Marathi in Goa and Gujarati in Daman and Diu,[27] the statehood issue acquired a new and curious momentum. New Delhi seemed anxious in 1987 to resolve a number of outstanding issues concerning union territories. After deciding to confer statehood on Arunachal Pradesh and Mizoram, there seemed little reason not to do the same for Goa. According to *The Hindu,* serious consideration for granting statehood to Goa 'coincided with the drubbing the Congress received in Kerala,' a result which left Goa as the party's only government in the south.[28]

In a move characterized by unanimity and ad hocism, Parliament on May 30, 1987 passed two separate bills including a constitutional amendment to achieve the result. The Reorganization Bill conferred statehood on Goa and formed a new union territory comprising Daman and Diu, while the 57th Amendment provided for a forty-member Assembly for the new state.[29] Goa remained under the jurisdiction of the Bombay High Court and the lieutenant governor became the governor.

In retrospect, after a campaign that began in 1967 and included resolutions by the Assembly in 1971, 1976, 1983 and 1986, Goa's enhanced status appeared to come about almost too swiftly. No political party got what it wanted, as the Goa Congress had fought for Konkani with Roman script and the MGP had championed Marathi. In reality the issue was moot, as English was entrenched as the language of both education and administration.

Typically the Congress solution was a compromise which satisfied almost no one but the politicians, who used statehood as an opportunity to expand the size of both the legislature and the cabinet. Both developments added to an already costly governmental structure. Whereas there were 2,500 workers on the public payroll in Portuguese times, there are 45,000 now. The attainment of first class citizenship, while valued, was to prove expensive as federal assistance dropped significantly. Since union territories receive a 100 per cent grant from the centre compared to only a 30 per cent grant for a state, Goa was plunged into a financial crisis.[30] As eighty per cent of Goa's budget goes towards administrative expenditures, tax increases and civil servant allowance cutbacks were necessary to reduce a Rs 100 crore revenue gap.[31] Revenue was derived from increased sales taxes that realized Rs 210 crore—an inflationary and inadequate solution that placed the fiscal burden on the ordinary consumer—because business, including mine owners who export, are exempt from state or federal levies. As a consequence, 'Goans may end up as the most highly taxed people in the country.'[32]

The state's poor financial health necessitated an across-the-board twenty-five per cent cut in departmental budgets in February 1997. The cabinet also imposed a Rs 300 per person entry fee on foreign tourists on top of an existing twenty-five per cent luxury occupancy tax in a further effort to realize Rs two crore a year in revenue.[33] However, the levy proved counterproductive, as it created a perception that Goa was more expensive than resorts in neighbouring Kerala and Karnataka and contributed to a decline of between twenty per cent and forty per cent in hotel occupancy rates.[34]

As a result of heavy borrowing and consequent debt servicing, economists have complained that there are no funds available for economic development.[35] Indeed, the rate of increase in development expenditure has declined from 12.3 per cent per year in the early 1990s to under five per cent, while non-developmental expenditure has risen to 29.1 per cent in 1997–98 alone.[36] Having had the highest per capita income in the country during 1988–89—a figure inflated by remittances from abroad—Goa's all-India position has subsequently deteriorated. The state government has repeatedly argued that Goa deserves more federal assistance because of the contribution its mining and tourist industries make towards the nation's foreign exchange position. Nevertheless, in October 1990 Prime Minister V.P. Singh, claiming Goa was one of the country's 'better off states,' turned down a request that the jurisdiction be granted special category status making it eligible for the allotment of additional central funds.[37] Such a designation would have entitled Goa to a ninety per cent grant from the centre. As *Goa Today* lamented, the state is being 'penalised for the remarkable social progress it has made compared to the other states in the union. The very fact that [Goa] has a high per capita income, a low birth rate and literate populace goes against it in the allocation of funds from the centre.'[38]

Politics in the State of Goa

In the short term, the Rane government used the statehood issue to eke out a narrow victory over the MGP in the November 1989 elections. With the merger of the Goa Congress and the Indian National Congress, the 1989 campaign was essentially a two party race. In the straight fight the Congress won 40.52 per cent of the votes and eighteen seats, and the MGP captured an identical number of seats with 39.53 per cent of the votes (Table 5.1). Independents tipped the balance.

Table 5.1
Results of the 1989 Assembly Elections

Party	Candidates	Valid Votes	Percentage	Seats
MG	33	199,640	39.53	18
INC	40	204,321	40.52	18
Others	181	100,244	19.88	4
Total	254	504,205 out of 734,317 eligible	68.67	40

Source: *Assembly Elections Ready Reference 1994: 38–39.*

However, the loss of power by Rajiv Gandhi in Delhi in 1989 was a recipe for instability in the Congress-controlled states. By the following March, Rane's ten-year-old administration had been toppled by defectors who formed an unholy and unprincipled alliance of the most extreme elements from both the Catholic and Hindu communities.

In the face of a challenge by the nationalist Bharatiya Janata Party (BJP) to its Hindu base, the MGP began emphasizing its regional identity. As many Goans emigrate, education in English is regarded by them as a necessary prerequisite for foreign employment. Despite the body politic's clear cut preference for English,[39] the new MGP dominated government issued an order stopping grants to schools whose medium of instruction in the first to fourth standards was not the regional languages of Konkani or Marathi. The net effect of postponing English until the fifth standard was to denigrate that language and enhance Marathi.[40] The MG's unpopular actions in the Assembly jeopardized its future as a political party. The nationalist BJP's vigorous entry in the June 1991 elections divided the Hindu vote and enabled Congress to capture both of the state's parliamentary seats.

Political Instability

Whereas between 1963 and 1989 Goa had only three chief ministers, in the following year it had four different men occupy that office.

Rane was followed in March 1990 by the controversial Churchill Alemao,[41] who was sworn in as interim chief minister until Speaker Luis Proto Barbosa could replace him on April 14. Barbosa, whose administration was tainted by charges of corruption, was disqualified from membership in the state Assembly for violating the anti-defection statute in December 1990. Instead of calling for new elections as had happened in 1979, Governor Khurshed Alam Khan suspended the Assembly until he appointed MG leader Ravi Naik as chief minister on January 25, 1991. Although disqualified by the speaker under the anti-defection law, Naik was able to govern with Congress support when party leader Dr Wilfred de Souza was named deputy chief minister. The latter became chief minister in May 1993 when the High Court upheld Naik's disqualification. Restored to the legislature in February 1994, Naik attempted to regain his former position. When Governor Bhanu Prakash Singh dissolved the de Souza ministry and reinstalled Naik in April of that year, the governor was dismissed by the centre for behaving unconstitutionally. New Delhi reinstated de Souza until the pending state Assembly elections. Hence, within a single legislative term, India's newest state had changed governments four times and chief ministers seven times.[42]

Rane Restored: The 1994 Assembly Elections

These manoeuvres rewarded defectors and increased the cost of government, while undermining the public's faith in the political system. Various expansions of the cabinet raised its membership to fourteen, one for every 50,000 voters. What the public wanted from its government was hard working MLAs who provided basic amenities like power, water and roads, not self-serving behaviour.[43] Indignation at the machinations of the state's legislators was registered in the 1994 elections when voter turnout increased from its 1989 level of 68.7 per cent to 70 per cent. The 1994 elections failed to produce a majority in the forty-member state legislature, as the Congress garnered eighteen seats, the MGP won twelve and its alliance partner, the Bharatiya Janata Party, carried four constituencies (see Table 5.2). Significantly, in 1994 the voters rejected eighteen sitting MLAs, as they punished defectors who had formed the Popular Front government. Among the casualties was highly regarded long-time MGP leader Ramakant Khalap,

Table 5.2
Results of the 1994 Assembly Elections

Party	Candidates	Valid Votes	Percentage	Seats
MG	25	128,033	21.86	12
INC	40	216,165	36.91	18
BJP	12	52,094	8.89	4
UGDP	20	47,765	8.16	3
Others	214	141,654	24.18	3
Total	311	585,711 out of 822,830 eligible	71.18	40

Source: Results provided by the Office of the Election Commissioner, Panaji.

whose reputation had been tainted by his association with the coalition government in which he had served as deputy chief minister. In their house-cleaning the electorate also vanquished potential chief minister Francisco Sardinha as well as numerous other former Congress cabinet members.

That the voters also punished the state's parties is evidenced by the fact that even though they formed an alliance, the BJP–MGP's combined total of 30.75 per cent of the votes represented a decline of almost ten per cent from 1989. Congress' share of the votes also dropped from its previous level by 3.61 per cent to 36.91 per cent. Part of the fall in the Congress total was attributable to a split in the Catholic vote. After the Congress failed to give Churchill Alemao a berth in spite of readmitting all other defectors, he formed his own party under the banner United Goan Democratic Party (UGDP). In what later appeared ironical, sitting MP Eduardo Faleiro strongly supported giving the Congress endorsement to Alemao in Benaulim in order to protect its own position in South Goa,[44] while the Rane faction of the party was adamantly opposed to his reinstatement. Rane was supported by Prime Minister P.V. Narasimha Rao who had initiated his party's national election campaign in Goa in November 1994 and who now intervened in the allocation of Congress tickets. His interference caused a number of potential nominees to run as independents and provoked a backlash against the 'high command' politics of the national parties. As a result, independents polled 22.1 per cent of the votes and won three seats. Their competition split the Congress votes, and that party was unable to carry the state's four largest cities. The UGDP which captured 8.16 per cent of the votes seriously eroded Congress support in the southern *taluka* of Salcette, as Alemao and two associates were elected. It was reported that Dr Wilfred de Souza was using the UGDP to defeat potential rivals for the chief ministership like Francisco Sardinha.[45] While de Souza succeeded in accomplishing that objective, many of his own supporters were consumed in the crossfire, and those Congressmen who survived were not disposed to select him as chief minister.

As a consequence, Pratapsingh Rane, with the support of three independents and four MGP defectors, was able in 1994 to regain the office he had held for more than ten years and form a Congress-led government. After fifteen months Rane engineered a further defection from the three-member UGDP group—an act that was to have repercussions for the 1996 parliamentary elections.

The Politics of Revenge: The 1996 Parliamentary Elections

Politics in Goa has become the settling of scores. De Souza was not satisfied with the position of deputy chief minister, which he regarded as a demotion. He blamed the two sitting Congress MPs for insisting that a Hindu be chosen as a chief minister in a state where Hindus had increased to sixty-seven per cent of Goa's population and Christians had declined to twenty-six per cent prior to the 1996 campaign.[46] As a result he virtually sat out that contest, speaking only once for the party nominees during the campaign.[47] He attributed the Congress' defeat to a drop in the turnout by Catholic voters who refused to exercise their franchise because of the shabby way the Congress had treated him after the 1994 Assembly elections,[48] a theory the *Herald* called 'fanciful' since turnout in the state increased substantially from 43 per cent in 1991 to 56.5 per cent in 1996.[49]

By denying the incumbent Harish Zantye renomination for the traditionally MGP North seat at the last moment, the Congress also guaranteed the sitting member's enmity. His designated successor, Amrut Kansar, a recycled former MGP MP who had been elected only once in 1977, was a weak candidate who had little chance against the well-known Ramakant Khalap in the traditional Maharashtrawadi Gomantak stronghold. Voters in the northern parliamentary constituency appeared eager to reverse the defeat they had inflicted upon the MGP party leader in the 1994 Assembly elections. Consequently Khalap was sent to Delhi by a margin of 10,545 votes.

Alemao secured his revenge against the Congress by opposing his former mentor Eduardo Faleiro, the highly regarded five-term incumbent for the South (Mormugao) seat. After initially backing Francisco Sardinha, Alemao declared his candidacy for the post on March 10. At first the notion of a man indicted on criminal charges contesting the minister of state for chemicals and fertilizers evoked ridicule. The state's leading newspaper called Alemao 'the most hated man in Salcette.'[50] Not surprisingly, Faleiro attempted to brand his challenger as uneducated, unqualified and tainted by corruption.

While Alemao's campaign was originally dismissed as having only a nuisance quality[51] against a politician of stature, he succeeded in depicting the aloof Faleiro as being a Delhi elite who was out of touch with the problems of the state's downtrodden. Alemao's campaign—which employed rock bands at his rallies—was in sharp contrast to Faleiro's lacklustre speeches that emphasized experience at a time incumbency was a liability.[52] Appeals to 'vote for the candidate who has brought honour and glory to Goa'[53] did not resonate among the electorate at a time when unemployment was their principal concern.[54] The longer Faleiro campaigned, the smaller his crowds became. He even neglected to show up for his own rally in the important city of Ponda.[55] Faleiro's effort to reach out to women voters was seriously damaged by the loss of his wife who had been an effective campaigner, in a November 1993 traffic accident. Moreover, the Catholic Church, which had supported Eduardo Faleiro in past campaigns in a district that was forty per cent Christian, issued circulars which criticized him for supporting the Konkan railway because it would allegedly inundate Goa with mainly Hindu outsiders.[56] By contrast, Churchill promised, if elected, to ensure that more Goans were employed in the line's construction—a commitment that did not hurt him in Mormugao *taluka* which has a large number of immigrants.

Alemao's campaign especially resonated with young voters who became an important vote bank. Because of his sponsorship of sporting activities, he was well known to the 14,000 new voters aged eighteen to twenty-two who were added to electoral rolls that had expanded from 409,000 to 481,621 in five years. In the entire state the electorate had expanded by 100,000 since 1991. The 72,621 voters who had been added to the electoral rolls in South Goa—mostly Hindus from outside the state—had no attachment to Eduardo Faleiro. Even though Alemao cleverly emphasized preserving Goan identity and used the 'two leaves' anti-merger with Maharashtra symbol from the 1967 Opinion Poll, he was careful to court the non-Christian Hindu voters.[57] An OBC he also played the caste card against his Brahman opponent and, in the process, appealed to many low caste Hindu voters whom the incumbent ignored. Churchill's appeal to that community would be reflected in his impressive showing in Hindu majority districts like Ponda. Instead of Alemao's alleged criminal ties to the Bombay–Dubai mafia being a liability, his 'Don image' became an asset. It was suggested that Alemao's shady connections and generous personal spending would enable him to get things done for Goa. By mid-April it was recognized by the press that 'Eduardo faces an uphill battle.'[58] Faleiro's predicament was aggravated by the national tide against the Congress during the last week of the campaign and his opponent's promise to support a United Front government. Not even a widely circulated 'public call to right thinking citizens' signed by a cross section of Goa's establishment[59] just prior to the May 2 poll could save the incumbent. As a result of emphasizing his caste, class, generational and regional differences with his opponent, Alemao swamped Faleiro by over 25,000 votes, more than double the margin the popular Ramakant Khalap ran up against a weak candidate in the North.[60] Moreover, his 109,000 total votes exceeded by 8,893 the previous record 100,453 ballots Faleiro had polled in the South Goa district in 1984.

The extent of Eduardo Faleiro's defeat was pervasive. His opponent won votes from not merely MGP and BJP supporters, but also traditional backers of the Congress. Faleiro's vote fell dramatically in every Assembly district (see A. Rubinoff 1997b for details). The UGDP candidate secured 40.17 per cent of the votes, while Faleiro managed only 30.88 per cent—a drop of more than twenty-six percentage points from his previous contest. Faleiro's vote fell by 37.75 per cent in his heavily Catholic home *taluka* of Salcette, leading one analyst to conclude that the Congress' sole remaining base in Goa is in areas where Christians are a decisive minority.[61]

The double-barrelled defeat in Goa which left the state devoid of Congress representation in the Lok Sabha for the first time since 1971, and the party's debacle throughout the country placed the Rane government in jeopardy. There was speculation that it would be toppled as had happened in 1990 after Rajiv Gandhi lost power in Delhi.[62] However, because of the way his rivals behaved during the campaign, it was difficult to pin the blame for the Congress' debacle on the chief minister. Faleiro's effort was sabotaged by other Congress politicians who, as in 1994, engaged in 'fratricidal warfare' that undermined their candidates' campaigns in both of Goa's districts. According to the *Herald*, Congress MLAs acted like 'many Brutuses'[63] and made appearances at their opponents' rallies. Sardinha, upset that the man who defeated him in 1994 had been invited into the Congress, was accused of 'going through the motions for Faleiro.'[64] One cabinet member even participated in ceremonies opening Churchill's brother's restaurant in Margao during the middle of the campaign. In any event, the unstable situation in Delhi prevented Rane's immediate removal.

The 1994 assembly and 1996 parliamentary elections revealed that all parties contain factions that appear to be more interested in defeating intra-party rivals than the formal opposition. Just as they had cooperated in removing Rane in 1990, de Souza, Churchill, and Khalap worked together in the 1994 and 1996 elections. By remaining in the Congress, de Souza was the linchpin of the triumvirate which one newspaper dubbed as the 'Churchill–Khalap–Willy Axis.'[65] Double-dealing, however, was not restricted to the Congress. Sensing it was losing its Hindu base to the BJP, the MGP was unwilling to renew its 1994 alliance with that national party in 1996. Nevertheless, some of the BJP's supporters worked against their own nominees on behalf of regional party candidates to defeat the Congress candidates in Goa, because they wanted to deny it power in Delhi.[66] As a result, the BJP obtained only 11.5 per cent of the South Goa votes compared to the 13.6 per cent it won in 1991. However, BJP supporters were unwilling to continue their cooperation with the MG and the UGDP after the election. There was especially close cooperation during the 1996 parliamentary election between the MG, which was strong in the mainly Hindu North, and the UGDP, whose base was in the largely Christian areas of the Southern district. MGP voters who had defected to Alemao caused Dr Kashinath Jalmi, the party's candidate in South Goa and its leader in the Assembly, to forfeit his deposit. As a result of the collapse of its support, the MGP's share of the vote declined from 20.8 per cent to 13.38 per cent.

Speculation that MG–UGDP cooperation would lead to a new regional party[67] was short-lived. When Prime Minister Deve Gowda named Ramakant Khalap as his minister of state for law, justice and company affairs, the appointment earned the resentment of Churchill Alemao who had hoped to be designated sports minister.[68] As Goa is too small a state to have both of its MPs included in the council of ministers, the ambitions of Khalap and Alemao collided. Hence, any talk of forming a new regional party that would be more responsive to the Goans than either the national BJP or Congress was, ironically, stifled by developments in Delhi.

What happened in Goa in the 1996 elections reflected the national pattern: voters opted for regional parties to protest Congress misrule, corruption, and indifference. However in India's smallest state as elsewhere, they did not turn towards the BJP, but instead gravitated towards regional parties. In South Goa, as elsewhere in India, they replaced a long-serving incumbent of stature with a vernacular politician who was himself tainted.[69]

Clearly statehood has not enhanced Goa's political stability or the public's esteem for the Legislative Assembly. Mirroring the situation in New Delhi, self-serving politicians in Goa are manoeuvering for personal gain and position instead of promoting the public interest (deSouza 1996b). After the 1996 parliamentary elections Chief Minister Pratapsingh Rane induced the defection of another UGDP MLA into the Congress, leaving Churchill Alemao's brother Joachim as the party's solitary MLA. The tactic means that the Congress is dependent on defectors for a quarter of its majority, while the UGDP—despite being a vehicle for underemployed young people to express their discontent in the 1996 parliamentary elections—has been exposed as a family affair. Clearly the recent shifts of legislators have obliterated the state's existing political delineations. Moreover, the rampant defections and the criminalization of politics have undermined the public's faith in Goa's political system.[70]

As was the case with every member of parliament from the Panaji constituency, Ramakant Khalap was unable to secure re-election in 1998. Instead of being the beneficiary of a protest vote, as happened in 1996, the central government minister was the target of the voters' unhappiness with the unstable political situation in India. The rivalry between Alemao and Khalap caused both the incumbents to be defeated in 1998, enabled the Congress to recapture both seats with a declining plurality in a four-cornered race, and provided an opportunity for an impressive surge in BJP support in the state. Whereas the local parties had cooperated in 1996, Alemao ran a UGDP candidate against Khalap for the North seat in 1998. Alemao's surrogate finished fourth, but contributed to a decline of more than 30,000 in Khalap's total vote and caused the MGP candidate to fall to third place. Moreover, the intervention in the North dissipated Alemao's resources in his own district. Alemao polled 20,000 fewer votes than in 1996 and also finished third. The beneficiaries of the regional parties' conflict were the state units of the national organizations. The BJP came within 583 votes of winning the North seat which was claimed for the Congress by former chief minister Ravi Naik even though the total votes for the Congress in the district declined by over 13,000. While Francisco Sardinha retook the Mormugao constituency, the BJP candidate trailed by only 7,850 votes and finished a strong second. The MGP—many of whose workers defected to the BJP—was obliterated in the South, polling only 8,653 votes. The MG's dismal showing cast doubts on its future viability as a political party. Although the Congress recaptured the state's two parliamentary seats, it lost a majority of the Assembly districts. By contrast, the BJP tripled its support in the South and nearly doubled it in the North. Its performance in 1998 assured that the BJP would be in a strong position for the 1999 Assembly elections and beyond.

In an earlier writing (A. Rubinoff 1983), I concluded that the pattern of post-liberation politics in the former Portuguese territories seemed to reinforce the findings of those social scientists who believe that while the impact of the process of modernization initially causes issues to be expressed in communal terms, such sectarian conflict eventually generates interest groups, political parties and other institutions that penetrate the body politic and promote national integration. The manner in which Goa achieved statehood in 1987 suggests that Indian politicians are not averse to reviving communal issues, such as language, in order to obtain selfish objectives. What is unique in the Goan case is that it was the minority Christian community that risked bloodshed by taking the initiative. As was the situation during the 1967 Opinion Poll, the Christians made common cause with the Hindu Brahman community in order to promote the Konkani language. What is regrettable is that twenty-five years after territorial integration, the Government of India responded to violence and not democratic politics in granting statehood.

What statehood has done is put the onus on the dominant local Congress party to govern effectively, and deprived it of the opportunity to blame Delhi for its inability to produce results. As is the situation nationally, the Congress in Goa continues to fragment. Its only reliable base is Catholic voters in the outlying New Conquests, where they are a minority (deSouza 1996a). The entry of the BJP—another national party—has temporarily worked to the INC's advantage by splitting the opposition vote in a plural electoral system. Whether the BJP has staying power or, as has been suggested,[71] is a temporary phenomenon in Goa comparable to the Janata Party in the 1970s, remains to be determined. As more Hindus from other parts of India migrate to Goa, its base is likely to grow. The BJP's task in Goa is to replicate its successes in neighbouring Karnataka and Maharashtra, rather than its failure in Kerala. As the BJP's appeal is largely to educated youths who are abundant in Goa, it is likely in the long run to displace the MGP whose base of Marathi-speaking rural illiterates is dying.

In any event, as is the case elsewhere in India, it is becoming virtually impossible to form a government in Goa, let alone govern. The 1994 elections demonstrated the inability of any single party to govern Goa independently. In order to form a government, any party—the Congress included—has to manufacture defections or forge an unstable coalition. This lack of performance has revived the prospects of regional parties, but also dramatically increased the proportion of votes secured by independent candidates. Political instability, as Samuel Huntington (1968) suggests, is hardly a formula for either economic development or political integration.

END NOTES

1. *The Times of India* (New Delhi), November 13, 1965.
2. Legislative Assembly of Goa, Daman and Diu, Debates, Typescript, October 10, 1976, p. 128.

3. *The Hindustan Times* (New Delhi), November 18, 1978, p. 5.
4. Interview, New Delhi, July 5, 1979.
5. *Navhind Times* (Panaji), March 19, 1969.
6. Ibid., September 14, 1970.
7. Ibid., February 17, 1971.
8. *Legislative Assembly of Goa, Daman and Diu, Debates*, Vol. VIII, No. 2, February 12, 1971, p. 69 and No. 11, March 26, 1971, p. 473.
9. *Navhind Times*, September 23, 1971.
10. Ibid. March 10, 1976.
11. Legislative Assembly of Goa, Daman and Diu, Debates, Typescript, October 10, 1976.
12. Statement by Dr Wilfred de Souza, president, Goa Congress Committee. *Navhind Times*, May 26, 1977.
13. Interview, Panjim, January 1, 1980.
14. Interview with D. Mandal, minister of state for home affairs, New Delhi, November 11, 1978.
15. *Navhind Times*, February 18, 1971.
16. Ibid., March 8, 1972.
17. *Statesman Weekly*, June 4, 1977, p. 15.
18. *The Times of India* (New Delhi), November 16, 1978, p. 15.
19. A resolution to this effect was initially defeated in the Assembly in 1971, *Legislative Assembly of Goa, Daman and Diu, Debates*, Vol. VIII, No. 27, · April 23, 1971, p. 1529, but others have subsequently met with more success as it became politically expedient for all parties to endorse such legislation. The objective was achieved on August 20, 1992 when both houses of Parliament unanimously passed the 78th Amendment to the Constitution.
20. *Navhind Times*, March 24, 1980.
21. *The Hindu* (International Edition), August 17, 1985.
22. Legislative Assembly of Goa, Daman and Diu, Debates, Typescript, February 2, 1987.
23. *India Today*, January 15, 1987, p. 29.
24. *Goa Today*, January 1987, p. 20.
25. *India Today*, January 31, 1987, p. 33.
26. *Goa Today*, January 1987, p. 3.
27. Legislative Assembly of Goa, Daman and Diu, Debates, Typescript, February 2, 1987.
28. *The Hindu* (Madras), May 30, 1987.
29. Government of Goa, *Official Gazette*, July 9, 1987.
30. Satyendra S. Naik, 'Slipping into a Fiscal Morass,' *Goa Today*, February 1992, pp 12–20.
31. *Goa Today*, June 1987, p. 24.
32. 'Ten Years of Statehood,' *Goa Today*, June 1997, p. 3.
33. *India News Network Digest*, Vol. 2, Issue 1392, February 9, 1997. <editor@ind-net.org> (February 10, 1997).
34. Devika Sequeira,'Goa: Tourists Now Find It Less Attractive,' *Deccan Herald News Service*, India News Network Digest, Vol.2, Issue 1435, February 19, 1997. <editor@indnet.org> (February 20, 1997).

35. I am grateful to Professor Errol D'Souza, Department of Economics, Goa University for providing me with documentation on these matters in February 1994.
36. 'Budget Blues', *Goa Today*, March 1998.
37. *Goa Today*, November 1990, p. 60.
38. *Goa Today*, June 1997, p. 3.
39. 'Speak Konkani, Want English,' *Herald* (Panaji), May 23, 1991.
40. 'Fooling with the Schooling,' *Goa Today*, July 1990, pp 12–20.
41. Alemao's brother Alvernaz was killed by customs agents, and the former chief minister was arrested on a charge of smuggling on May 16. 1991, *Herald*, May 17, 1991. In a series of bizarre events, a customs agent was incarcerated and Alemao and two other brothers were released on a technicality. *Goa Today*, November 1991. Alemao, who was denied the Congress ticket, was returned to the Assembly by a landslide vote from the Benaulim constituency in the 1994 elections. He faces a Rs one crore fine on the smuggling charge. *Herald*, December 8, 1994, p. 1.
42. 'An Unending Maze,' *Goa Today*, March 1994, p. 9.
43. *Navhind Times* (Panaji), November 1 and November 12, 1994.
44. Ibid., December 19, 1994, and December 6, 1994, p. 1.
45. *Gomantak Times*, October 11, 1994, p. 1., and *Navhind Times* December 28, 1994, p. 1.
46. Interview, Panjim, June 12, 1996.
47. In his defense De Souza produced a letter from Chief Minister Pratapsingh Rane dated April 23, 1996, instructing MLAs to concentrate on their own constituency.
48. *Herald*, May 4, 1996, p. 1.
49. Ibid., May 17, 1996, p. 4.
50. *Navhind Times*, March 11, 1996.
51. Peter Ronald deSouza, 'Community Factor Matters,' *Frontline*, April 19, 1996, pp 46–47.
52. *Goa Today*, May 1996, pp 18–26.
53. *Gomantak Times*, April 28, 1996, p. 1.
54. Ibid., April 24, 1996.
55. *Goa Today*, May 1996, p. 25.
56. *Navhind Times*, May 1, 1996, p. 1.
57. Ibid., April 17, 1996, p. 3 and April 18, 1996, p. 4.
58. Ibid., April 19, 1996, p. 1.
59. *Gomantak Times*, April 30, 1996, p. 1.
60. Peter Ronald deSouza, 'Goa: A Vote against Misgovernance,' *Frontline*, June 14, 1996, pp 100–01.
61. Peter Ronald deSouza, '1996 Elections: A Protest Against the Congress,' *Navhind Times* (Panaji), June 3 and·12, 1996, cf [Parker], 'Congress Base Intact,' *Navhind Times*, June 10, 1996.
62. M. Madan Mohan, 'Congress (I) Drubbed in Goa,' *Frontline*, May 31, 1996, pp 130–31.
63. *Herald*, May 10, 1996, p. 4.
64. Ibid., May 1, 1996, p. 4.

65. *Navhind Times*, April 13, 1996. Khalap ensured de Souza's reelection to the Assembly from Saligao by running a Shiv Sena candidate against him in his constituency, and de Souza attempted to return the favour by opposing him with a weak candidate in Mandrem—a strategy which did not work in 1994.
66. On this point see Ibid., April 29, 1996, p. 23, and M. Madan Mohan, 'The Tale of Two MPs,' *The Hindu* (Madras), June 10, 1996, p. 17.
67. Made by Peter Ronald deSouza in the *Navhind Times*, June 2 and 3, 1996.
68. *Statesman*, July 8, 1996, p. 9.
69. See *India Today*, July 15, 1996 for a discussion of indicted criminals who were elected to Parliament.
70. According to polls conducted by Goa University political scientist Peter Ronald deSouza for the *Herald* in May 1991.
71. Chandrakant Keni, 'Need for a Regional Party,' *Goa Today*, May 1995, pp 46–49.

Chapter 6

Patterns of Integration Since 1961

◆

Although typically the nationalist movement in a developing country such as India is an integrating agent (LaPalombara and Weiner 1966; cf. Coleman and Rosberg 1964), it was the army that brought Goa into the Indian Union, and it is immigration which is transforming the former Portuguese possessions. The Congress party was initially unable to play the role in Goa it had elsewhere in India. Its lack of historical roots in Goa and the rivalry of its Maharashtra and Mysore wings, repeatedly denied the Congress electoral success in a communal setting. In the first territorial elections its ideology of secularism clashed with existing primordial loyalties.

The task of integrating Goans into the country initially divided them instead. The failure of both Catholics and Hindus to struggle together in a mass nationalist movement created a leadership vacuum that politicians in other states attempted to fill. During the 1960s the non-Brahman Hindus promoted merger with Maharashtra. Their vehicle in this endeavour was the Maharashtrawadi Gomantak Party. Although it claimed to be an integrating agent, by promoting regional as opposed to national integration, the MGP's campaigns for merger with Maharashtra, in fact, exacerbated sectarian differences. However, the Opinion Poll in 1967 forced those Catholics, who had gravitated to the United Goans Party in an attempt to prevent the dilution of their community's distinct culture, to cooperate with the nationalist Hindu Brahmans who traditionally supported the Congress. Following the failure of the merger campaign, it became permissible for Hindu Goans to emphasize their local identity by voting for the regional party and against the

Congress. Yet, over time, national political parties became a factor in Goa. Ironically, the intrusion of the national organizations split the opposition vote in 1977 and maintained the regional party in office longer than otherwise would have been the case. Since it came to power in the 1980 elections, it has been the Congress, as the dominant party in a plurality electoral system, that has benefited from a divided opposition. Once it attained power the Congress acted as an integrating agent on behalf of the union government. It was the Congress—a national party—which obtained statehood for Goa in 1987 and completed Goa's integration into the Indian Union.

As the ruling party, the Congress has assumed responsibility for governing Goa and overseeing its development. Expansion of education and the development of the region after the attainment of statehood have made the performance of the government, instead of communal concerns, as the principal electoral issue. This does not mean that issues of integration have disappeared from Goan politics. It is now the influx of migrants from other parts of India which has replaced merger with Maharashtra as the principal social concern. Politicians have revived sectarian issues in order to avoid discussing the consequences of development. Politics in Goa have come to replicate the all-India pattern of defections and unstable governments.

Goa's economic development has been more noteworthy than its record of political stability. Given the former Portuguese colony's late incorporation into the Indian Union, Goa's economic achievements are especially impressive. India has been integrating Goa while the country was undergoing its own experience of development. Unlike the rest of the country, Goa has had a conscious development policy only since 1962–63. By that time the Indian republic was halfway into its Third Plan. Most of Goa's administrative and economic reforms were initiated in 1964–65, but their implementation awaited the outcome of the 1967 Opinion Poll which determined the territory's discrete status (see National Council of Applied Economic Research 1970). Even then the party which had proposed merger with Maharashtra did not seem to stress the territory's development. During the entire sixteen years when it was in office the MGP spent only Rs 192 crores of central funds earmarked for development and even returned moneys to the national exchequer (an action that Fernandes [1997: 53] claims is 'unparalled' in the history of any state), while the Congress claimed that it had spent as much as Rs 226 crores in its first five years in office (Esteves 1986: 205). In reality, planning for long-range economic development began in Goa only with the Fourth Plan. Goa has made major strides in economic development since then. The net state domestic product (NSDP) at current prices grew from Rs 27 crores in 1960 to Rs 315 crores in 1980–81. During the 1980s the NSDP grew at an average rate of 20.26 per cent to reach Rs 954 crores in 1990–91. At constant prices the per capita annual income grew from Rs 3,145 in 1980–81 to Rs 4,119 in 1990–91, an increase of 31 per cent. However, this rapid development has been characterized by an absence of vision and a catering to special interests. Consequently, as will be shown, it has produced a transformation in Goa that has engendered backlashes and dislocations.

The Transformation of Goa

Integration, as Robert Newman (1984) has pointed out, has transformed Goa. In contrast to the situation that pertained under Portuguese rule, there is now a high level of social development in Goa, reflected by its high literacy, low birth rate, improving health care, and impressive educational facilities (see Pai Panandiker and Chaudhuri 1983). Goa has achieved the distinction of having 'the best physical quality of life . . . in the country' (Goa Chamber of Commerce & Industry 1992: 1)[1] measured by such indicators as: per capita income, level of literacy, per capita power consumption, birth rate, death rate, infant mortality rate, maternal mortality rate, doctor–population ratio, road length per thousand sq. kms, motor vehicles per 100,000 people, and the ratio of population per banking office.

Education

Practically non-existent under the Portuguese, education has expanded rapidly since liberation. This has had a dramatic effect on literacy rates and accounts for the fact that the state with a population of 1.4 million has eight daily newspapers in three languages. Whereas only about a third of Goans were literate in 1961, over three-quarters are today. The number would be higher, were it not that only sixty per cent of outsiders who reside in the state are literate compared to ninety per cent of native born Goans.

Under Portuguese rule there had been only 476 primary schools and 119 secondary schools. Higher education consisted of one Lyceum, one pharmacy school, and one medical college. By 1991, 1,266 primary schools, 338 secondary schools and 43 institutions at the tertiary level, including a university, were in existence. Goa's noted industrialists, under the guise of posing as philanthropists, have created colleges named after them, leaving the government to bear the costs of their operation. Consequently, whereas about 50,000 students were enrolled in Portuguese times, the total now exceeds a million. There are currently over 17,000 university students, more than can be absorbed into the state's workforce. Each year an additional 15,000 new jobs must be created in an economy that already has over 100,000 unemployed. Unemployment has become the principal concern of the increasingly educated electorate.[2] It is among this segment of the population that the ruling party, as was the case with its predecessor, is losing support.

The Economy

Significant economic advances, especially in the areas of industry, agriculture, fishing, mining, and tourism, have been made since 1961. Goa's economy has been transformed from an import-oriented economy supported by exports of mineral ore to one sustained by service industries. By 1993–94 the state domestic product exceeded Rs 1,400 crore, and the share of agriculture had declined to fifteen per cent, compared to thirty-five per cent for industry, and fifty per cent for service industries[3] (see Table 6.1 for the major indices of economic change in Goa). Government loans fostered such industries as pesticides, fertilizers, pharmaceuticals, barge-building and the brewing of beer.

Goa is the only state in the Indian Union where agriculture accounts for less than thirty per cent of the economy. Agriculture has been described as the 'weak link' in the economy (Angle 1983: 17). Even though 43.20 per cent of the state's area is under cultivation, only about 24 per cent of the working population are engaged in agriculture; this compares with 60 per cent in colonial times. Whereas the region produced enough food to feed itself for eight months a year in Portuguese times, due to population growth today it grows only enough to be self-sufficient for three months. Despite its relative decline (see Goa Chamber of Commerce &

Table 6.1
Indices of Change

Year	1961	1971	1981	1991
POPULATION	627,000	795,000	1,003,141	1,169,000
Decennial growth rate	5.14	36.88	26.16	16.53
Per cent Christian	36.8	NA	NA	28
Per cent literate	35.41	51.96	65.71	76.96
Per cent urban	14.81	25.56	32.03	41
NET STATE DOMESTIC PRODUCT				
(IN CRORES)	27		315	954
Per cent in manufacturing	7.3			24.7
Number of factories	34	142	186	272
Food production				
(in tons)	58,000			143,000
Tons of fish caught	1,700	39,980	31,502	53,178
Trawlers	4		600	985
Bank branches	2	60(1968)	298	305
Hotel beds	1,736	1,866	6,587	12,650
Motor vehicles	8,531	11,710	35,625	125,965
MINERAL PRODUCTION				
(In '000 tons)				
Iron	6,395	10,235	11,951	13,554
Manganese	49	5	4	11
Ferro manganese ore	122	203	113	44
Bauxite		46	30	7
Total	6,566	10,489	12,098	13,616
INFRASTRUCTURE				
Villages electrified	3	127	343	386
Per capita electrical				
consumption (in KW)	13		283	406.37
EDUCATION				
Schools				
Primary (I–IV)				
Enrolment	43,244	98,207	122,470	105,173
Middle (V–VII)	–	365	371	440
Enrolment	–	42,306	66,956	83,708
Secondary (VIII–X)	119	193	246	338
Enrolment	9,511	31,507	45,593	60,908
Higher Secondary				
(XI–XII)	Nil	N.A.	17	43
Enrolment	Nil	N.A.	7,392	18,025
Vocational Schools	4	7	28	27
Enrolment	411	1,134	6,100	27
General Colleges	Nil	6	9	16
Enrolment	Nil	4,873	4,882	10,539
Professional Colleges	Nil	6	8	14
Enrolment	Nil	1,467	1,716	2,310

Source: Adapted from *Thirty Years of Economic Development in Goa 1961–1991*.

Industry 1992: 30), enormous strides have, nonetheless, been made in the agricultural sector since liberation was achieved. Food production has increased from 50,000 tons in Portuguese times to over 200,000 tons in the 1990s. By 1971 the production of rice, the region's principal crop, had increased by forty-five per cent as new land was brought under cultivation and existing irrigation canals improved. Increased yields were also registered in the production of coconuts, cashew nuts and the catch of fish. Farming, however, has become more a commercial and less of a subsistence family enterprise, as even small cultivators rely on daily labour. The large business houses, whose mine reserves are becoming depleted, have bought up agricultural land. Since commercial agriculturists pay their cultivators wages, they are exempt from the state's land-to-the-tiller legislation.

Fisheries play an important role in augmenting the food supply, as well as generating employment and foreign exchange. Goa's 104 kilometres coastline and 250 kilometres of inland waterways constitute one of the most extensive river systems in the country and are rich in resources. They support 21,000 people directly dependent on fishing and many more in related industries such as aquaculture. Four thousand hectares of low-lying lands that are used for paddy cultivation during the monsoon are farmed for fish and prawns the remainder of the year. The value of the 2,000 tons of prawns exported each year is about Rs six crores. The 1,700 tons harvested in colonial times has grown to 53,178 tons—out of an estimated potential yield of 70,000 tons. It is worth an estimated Rs twenty-three crores. The growth in the fish catch stems from a dramatic increase in the number of mechanized boats. Commercial trawlers, nearly non-existent in 1961, exceeded 900 by 1991. However, the number of registered vessels far exceeds those involved in fishing. Moreover, foreign factory ships are a drain on the local resources.

The manufacturing sector's share of the state's domestic product has grown from 7.3 per cent in 1960 to 24.7 per cent in 1990–91. In 1960–61 only sixty small scale industries, mostly engaged in food processing and handicrafts existed. In 1990–91 there were forty-two large and medium industries in the state. They employed nearly 10,000 persons and their total investment was Rs 221.78 crores. Another nearly 5,000 small scale industrial units, with an investment of Rs 90.34 crores, provided employment to over 30,000 workers. They produced a wide range of products, including: television sets, watches, auto parts, ceiling fans, nylon fishing nets, processed food, cotton yarn, liquor, fertilizers, pesticides, tires, drugs and processed sugar.

The Goa Chamber of Commerce and Industry (1992: 108) estimated that the mining industry and its related port activities account for more than a third of the state population's livelihood. Iron ore production rose from 6.4 million tons in the last year of Portuguese rule to a high of 14.8 million tons in 1976. It dropped to less than ten million tons in the 1980s and recovered to more than twelve million tons by 1990. Exports of iron ore, which stood at 0.38 lakh tons in 1961–62, increased to 133.60 lakh tons in 1990–91. The estimated foreign exchange earnings from that source were Rs 200 crores.

Extraction of bauxite and ferro manganese have declined more rapidly in recent years. Bauxite extraction declined from 167,000 tons in 1980–81 to 6,580 tons in 1990–91, and that of ferro manganese fell from 93,237 to 44,336 tons in the same period. As a result of the need to export ore, the port of Mormugao was expanded into one of the major harbours in western India. The Chapora, Mandovi, Sal and Zuari rivers form an inland waterway system that is extensively employed to transport minerals to the port. Nevertheless, since exports from its harbour far exceed imports to Goa, there is a recognition that the one way nature of the port is hampering the state's overall development. Consequently, there are demands that Mormugao be turned into a tariff free trading zone.[4] In March of 1997 as a means of stimulating shipping traffic, the state government opened the minor ports of Tiracol, Chapora, Panaji, Betual, and Talpona to private investment.

Remittances from abroad have compensated for the decline of revenue generated by the mining industry. The remittances from the 100,000 Goans—mainly Christians—who are in the Gulf are equivalent to the amount of money generated by the state's mining industry. While Hindus often resent this infusion of wealth earned abroad by Catholics, it is important to the state's economy. As the amount of money sent from foreign countries is considerable, there is vexation that the deposits are not invested locally by India's nationalized banks. Bank branches have increased from two in Portuguese times to 307. Their ratio to population of one branch for every 4,000 people, compared with the national average of one per 14,000, is the lowest in India. By 1994 their assets totalled Rs 2,836 crores, or an impressive Rs 24,000 per capita, providing an indication of the magnitude of local funds available for investment. The repatriation of remittances means that both in-migration and out-migration contribute to the rising price of property in the state.

Over a million tourists, twenty-five per cent from outside the country and 150,000 from Britain alone, come annually to enjoy the region's pristine beaches making the state the second most popular tourist destination for foreigners after Rajasthan.[5] Hotel beds which increased from 1,736 in 1961 to nearly 12,000 in 1990, rose dramatically to 21,000 in 1997, establishing Goa as the 'Hawaii of the sub-continent.' Ten five star hotels have located on its short coastline. Air service with the rest of the country continues to improve, and charter service with the Gulf and Europe is becoming commonplace. In fact Goa is the destination of fifty per cent of the country's chartered arrivals. Nevertheless, this traffic and a planned doubling of capacity is jeopardized by a paucity of cultural amenities and inadequate infrastructure.

Infrastructure

To accommodate the influx of tourists and business travellers, a new international airport is planned for the far north *taluka* of Pernem to replace the inadequate naval facility at Dabolim in the south. Thirty-five major bridges have been completed, but many including the Nehru bridge—which spans the Mandovi and connects Tiswadi with Bardez—have repeatedly been closed for repairs. The Zuari bridge, which made the remote southern districts accessible, was complete in December 1983, but by 1997 it too was under reconstruction.[6] Despite the decreased reliance on ferries, highway infrastructure in Goa remains inadequate. The number of buses has grown from sixteen regular size buses and 464 smaller *carreiras* as well as 635 taxis in Portuguese times to more than 1,000 buses and nearly 3,000 taxis. While transportation in the state is still difficult, the number of vehicles has increased from 8,531 to 131,481 in the thirty years since liberation. However, highway construction has not kept pace as the road surface has increased only from 2,735 mostly unpaved kilometres to 4,427 mostly asphalted kilometres.

Whereas, under the Portuguese the only railway was a narrow gauge track connecting Goa with Karnataka, a single-track broad gauge line linking Bombay to Mangalore in the Konkan regions of the south was opened in January 1998, and the South Central Railway's line to Londa in Karnataka is being converted to broad gauge to conform to the rest of the country. While indisputably an integrating agent, as the distance to Bombay will be shortened by 180 kilometers, the Konkan line's location in Goa has provoked controversy, particularly between the Hindu and Catholic communities.[7] The project—like the expansion of the Mormugao port—is seen by many as having little benefit for Goans, while at the same time increasing the number of outsiders in the state. Moreover, there is resentment that few Goans have been employed in building the line. At the same time, drainage problems associated with the railroad's construction have caused damage to many farms. Moreover, the aggravation associated with construction will have to be repeated if the line is made double-track. As a result of protests, principal cities such as Mapusa and Panjim will be deprived of rail service, while existing religious shrines in Old Goa will be in the shadow of the tracks. By the same token, rapidly developing regions, such as Bicholim and Ponda, will not be served by rail. Moreover, cost overruns and construction delays have caused freight and passenger fares to be approximately fifty per cent higher than comparable rates on lines elsewhere in India.

Under the Portuguese only three of Goa's villages had electricity. By 1991 the Indian government had electrified 377 of Goa's 386 villages and all fifteen towns, but power was not reliable; nor was every household electrified. The per capita consumption of electricity that was just 13 KWH in 1961 increased to 283 KWH in 1980–81 and reached 406.31 KWH in 1990–91. Goa must rely on Karnataka and Maharashtra for the generation of power. Moreover, a rapidly growing population competes for scarce resources with a rapidly expanding industrial sector. As is the situation elsewhere in India, inadequate infrastructure—especially the generation of electricity—is an impediment to development. Privatization is seen as a remedy to a Rs sixteen crore shortfall in power sector investment.

Backlashes

As one newspaper put it, Goa is 'a small state with big problems.'[8] The same forces that have advanced integration and promoted development have also created backlashes. The rapid expansion of electrification without a commensurate increase in generation has caused a severe shortage of power, and the growth in the number of industries and hotels has contributed to a corresponding water shortage. Development threatens to overwhelm the scenery that attracts tourists, as historic forts are transformed into luxury hotels that obscure beaches,[9] and buildings with Portuguese style architecture disappear. There is the threat of a mega theme park that would further transform the landscape. The state legislature has approved gaming in off-shore floating vessels, and the transformation of hotels into gambling casinos has already begun. The possibility that Goa will replicate Macao as another Las Vegas in Asia has generated fierce resistance from residents as the crime rate has soared and the number of murders averages between seventy and eighty a year. There are indications that the Bombay–Dubai mafia has established linkages in the state. Plans for intensified policing have met resistance from civil libertarians and opposition politicians.

Economic dislocations have sparked animosity between miners and farmers over pollution, landlords and tenants over agricultural rights, and traditional fishermen and trawler owners over the harvest of the sea (Newman 1981). The long-standing Zuari chemical plant operated since 1973 by Alcoa and U.S. Steel has always been controversial. A destructive invasion of nearby villagers protesting pollution by the Dupont Nylon 6, 6 tire plant at Keri in Ponda *taluka* in 1994[10] forced the relocation of the facility to Tamil Nadu where it also became a matter of controversy.

The new forms of economic activity and the new style of administration since 1961 have brought considerable numbers of non-Goan Indians and foreign tourists into the region. Foreigners are resented for their affluence and alien culture. Outsiders are blamed for the pervasiveness of drugs,[11] alcohol abuse,[12] and the spread of AIDS,[13] even though Goa has long been known for its consumption of liquor, has a reputation as a smugglers' haven, and has had high rates of venereal disease because of the brothels near the port of Mormugao.

More than any other factor, it is migration patterns between Goa and other parts of India that have promoted integration and threatened local identity. Attracted by Goa's high wage rate of Rs 100 per day, unskilled outsiders are pouring into Goa, while educated locals depart in search of white collar employment. Since

Goa's incorporation into India the population has more than doubled despite a considerable out-migration. Nearly 500,000—out of a 1991 total of 1,200,000—are migrants from other parts of India, and they are the fastest growing demographic segment. As a consequence of rapid unplanned growth, urbanization has nearly tripled from sixteen to forty-one per cent of the population in the thirty years since liberation. Urban sprawl, particularly in the larger cities of the Old Conquests, has resulted in deteriorating sanitation and living conditions. In the port city of Vasco da Gama an unauthorized shanty town of over 100,000 has been created. During rioting on November 1, 1982, over 100 huts were razed, and military and police detachments had to be sent to restore order.[14]

Such incidents of civil disorder, as well as the language riots of the mid-1980s, are evidence that economic development is, indeed, often associated with political decay (Huntington 1968). To some extent violence is the inevitable by-product of significant political and economic change. It is significant, that unlike the situation elsewhere in the country, it was the minority community—in this case the Christians—who demanded statehood to preserve their distinct culture within the broader Indian Union. Similarly, it was primarily that community that risked bloodshed to promote the Konkani language. However, it would be a mistake to associate such disturbances in Goa with the communal violence that plagues north India (see Jaffrelot 1996). There is no competition to define Goan identity. On the whole, Goans have, despite the efforts of politicians to sometimes exploit differences for short run political advantage, been appreciative of their diverse customs. Very few Hindus would blame Goan Catholics for the destruction of their temples by the Portuguese. Certainly, ethnic, religious, linguistic, caste and class differences can serve as a catalyst and energize disputes of all kinds. However as Brass (1996: 1) reminds, although it is tempting to attach political significance depending on the ethnic identities of the persons involved in what he (1997) calls collective violence, such alleged communal incidents are often the excuse to settle personal and familial scores (Tambiah 1996: 214, 261).

Just as in Portuguese times, emigration has served as an outlet for the discontented. It is estimated that there are currently 150,000 Goans—mainly Catholics—outside the Indian Union (Afonso 1995: 12). As educated Goans migrate to the Gulf and North America in search of better paying employment opportunities, local jobs increasingly fall to Indians from other parts of the country. While Goa's large business houses—the Chowgules, the Dempos, the Salgaonkars and the Timblos, already integrated into the world economy before liberation—have clearly profited from integration with India and the recent policy of economic liberalization, their expansion elsewhere has not created many jobs in Goa or for Goans. Ordinary Goans increasingly feel that they have not benefited from the region's development or its integration into the Indian Union. In response, the state government has committed itself to reserving 100 per cent of job vacancies for locals[15] and pressured private business through the use of subsidies to employ at least eighty per cent Goans in their establishments.[16] Common citizenship has come to coexist with regional citizenship as a prerequisite for employment.

Persons born in Goa before December 19, 1961 are now eligible for Portuguese passports and citizenship in the European Union, accelerating emigration. Since April 1994 there has been a Portuguese consulate in Panjim to process applicants. Although the indigenous Catholic population has particularly declined to twenty-six per cent of the state's total, most Goans have come to feel outnumbered in their own homeland. Indeed, if present population trends continue, Goans will be a minority in their own region by the end of the century.

Under the circumstances, it is difficult to see how more seats in the state legislature can benefit existing groups. Such tactics can only forestall the inevitable homogenization: In the long run, neither those who promote local nor regional identity will prevail. The influx from south India certainly makes it appear as if both sides lost the Opinion Poll.[17] There is a growing realization that Goa would have been less transformed had it been a neglected district of Maharashtra. While merger with Maharashtra was avoided, Goa is being submerged into the rest of the country. With each passing day, Goa becomes more like the rest of India—a reality that can be measured by the replacement of its decaying Mediterranean buildings with Indian style structures. The loss of its architectural and cultural uniqueness is the measure of Goa's integration. Ironically, Goans have a less distinctive identity now that their struggle for statehood has been completed. The attainment of statehood is only a reflection of the reality that politics in Goa—in contrast to other areas of India—has become more national (A. Rubinoff 1997a).

The increasing domination of state politics by the Indian National Congress and the BJP from New Delhi and the discrediting of the MGP have brought demands from some intellectuals that Goans should form a new regional party so that they might control their own destiny.[18] Yet, it is difficult to see how either sentimentalism by Hindu Brahmans or the identification of Goan culture with Catholicism can reverse the course of the region's evolution. What remains of the Lusitanian culture is largely being preserved for the benefit of tourists. An entire generation has come of age having known only Indian and not Portuguese rule. Hindus from other parts of India who have intermarried with locals have blended to create a new Indo-Goan identity and post-colonial culture that has in part replaced the Indo-Portuguese culture. Ironically, emigration, because of intermarriage with other Catholic ethnics, will also jeopardize the traditional Goan identity outside of India. Such changes reaffirm the proposition that the boundaries of ethnic groups are flexible (Tambiah 1996: 20–21), despite the fact that such collectivities continue to define themselves in a way that is 'permanently distinctive' (Horowitz 1985: 51). Communities, as Amitai Etzioni (1993) reminds, have a way of reinventing themselves. Hence, it is not only Goa but Goans who have changed since the incorporation into India in 1961.

As Jyotirindra Das Gupta (1997: 346) concludes, democratic participation in a power-sharing federal arrangement contributes to the successful integration of ethnic communities. Even though Goa's geographic and cultural situation made it relatively easy to incorporate and develop, its relatively smooth integration into India, is a reaffirmation of the country's democratic pluralist political system.

While what has happened to Goa is to some extent singular in world politics—occupation by fascist Portugal and integration with democratic India—the case has possible implications for other colonial enclaves that are being incorporated into China. The political and cultural experiences that Hong Kong and Macao undergo will be measured against what transpired in Goa. If their post-colonial experiences resemble the fate of Portugal's African possessions which saw a continuation of the repression of democratic freedoms, the unusualness of the Indian path of democratic development and integration will be underscored.

END NOTES

1. Most subsequent statistics are from this source.
2. *Gomantak Times*, April 24, 1996.
3. V.A. Pai Panandiker, 'A World to Win,' *Goa Today*, August 1995, pp 12–16.
4. See 'Free Port, Bane or Blessing?,' *Goa Today*, February 1992, pp 22–27.
5. *India Abroad*, November 24, 1995, p. 24.
6. *Goa Today*, May 1997, p. 47.
7. Ibid., March 1993.
8. *Herald* (Panaji), May 2, 1996, p. 4.
9. See *Goa Today*, January 1994, pp 8–9.
10. 'Contentious Issue,' *Goa Today*, November 1994, pp 10–11.
11. See *Goa Today*, May 1992.
12. 'Battling the Bottle,' *Goa Today*, December 1993, pp 10–13. Goa has over 600 bars, one for every 200 persons.
13. See *Goa Today*, April 1994, pp 12–22.
14. *The Hindu* (Madras), November 20, 1982, p. 15.
15. *Navhind Times* (Panaji), February 17, 1980.
16. *Goa Today*, May 1995, p. 20.
17. Chandrakant Keni in the *Navhind Times*, January 19, 1998, p. 5.
18. Chandrakant Keni, 'Need for a Regional Party,' *Goa Today*, May 1995, pp 46–49.

Appendices

Appendix I

Table 1

Party Outcome of Assembly Elections in Goa 1963–1994, by Constituency

Year	1963	1967	1972	1977	1980	1984	1989	1994
North Goa								
Pernem Taluka								
Mandrem	MGP	MGP	MGP	MGP	MGP	MGP	MGP	CONG
Pernem	MGP	MGP	MGP	MGP	MGP	CONG	MGP	MGP
Dargalim	NA	NA	NA	NA	NA	NA	NA	MGP
Bardez Taluka								
Tivim	MGP	MGP	MGP	MGP	CONG	CONG	MGP	CONG
Mapusa	MGP	MGP	MGP	MGP	CONG	MGP	MGP	MGP
Siolim	MGP	MGP	MGP	MGP	IND	MGP	MGP	MGP
Calangute	UG	UG	UG	MGP	CONG	MGP	CONG	CONG
Saligao	NA	NA	NA	NA	NA	NA	CONG	CONG
Aldona	UG	UG	UG	NA	NA	NA	MGP	CONG
Tiswadi Taluka								
Panaji	UG	UG	MGP	JP	IND	CONG	CONG	BJP
Taleigao	NA	NA	NA	NA	NA	NA	CONG	CONG

Santa Cruz	UG	UG	UG	JP	CONG	IND	CONG	IND
St Andre	UG	UG	UG	CONG	JP	CONG	IND	CONG
Cumbarjua	MGP	MGP	MGP	MGP	MGP	MGP	MGP	CONG
Bicholim Taluka								
Bicholim	MGP	MGP	MGP	MGP	IND	CONG	MGP	CONG
Maem	NA	NA	NA	NA	NA	NA	MGP	MGP
Pale	MGP	MGP	MGP	CONG	MGP	CONG	MGP	MGP
Satari Taluka								
Poriem	IND	MGP	MGP	CONG	CONG	CONG	CONG	CONG
Valpoi	NA	NA	NA	NA	NA	NA	CONG	BJP
South Goa								
Ponda Taluka								
Ponda	IND	MGP	MGP	MGP	CONG	MGP	MGP	MGP
Priol	NA	NA	NA	NA	NA	NA	MGP	MGP
Marcaim	MGP	MGP	MGP	MGP	MGP	MGP	MGP	BJP
Shiroda	MGP	MGP	MGP	MGP	CONG	CONG	CONG	CONG
Mormugao Taluka								
Mormugao	UG	UG	UG	CONG	CONG	CONG	CONG	IND
Vasco	NA	NA	NA	MGP	CONG	CONG	CONG	MGP
Cortalim	UG	UG	UG	CONG	CONG	CONG	CONG	CONG
Salcette Taluka								
Loutulim	NA	NA	NA	NA	NA	NA	CONG	CONG
Benaulim	UG	UG	UG	CONG	CONG	CONG	CONG	UGDP
Fatora	NA	NA	NA	NA	NA	NA	CONG	CONG
Margao	UG	UG	UG	CONG	CONG	CONG	IND	BJP
Curtorim	UG	UG	UG	CONG	CONG	CONG	CONG	UGDP
Navelim	UG	UG	UG	CONG	CONG	GC	CONG	CONG
Velim	NA	NA	NA	NA	NA	NA	CONG	IND
Cuncolim	UG	UG	UG	JP	CONG	CONG	CONG	UGDP

Continued

Year	1963	1967	1972	1977	1980	1984	1989	1994
Sanguem Taluka								
Sanvordem	NA	NA	NA	NA	NA	NA	MGP	MGP
Sanguem	MGP	MGP	MGP	MGP	CONG	CONG	MGP	CONG
Quepem Taluka								
Curchorem	MGP	MGP	MGP	MGP	CONG	MGP	CONG	CONG
Quepem	MGP	MGP	MGP	CONG	CONG	CONG	MGP	MGP
Canacona Taluka								
Canacona	MGP	MGP	MGP	MGP	CONG	CONG	MGP	CONG
Poingunim	NA	NA	NA	NA	NA	NA	CONG	MGP

Table 2
Results of the 1967 Opinion Poll in Goa

Constituency	No. of Voters	No. of Hindu Voters	%	Turn-out	%	Merger Vote	%	Union Territory Vote	%
Mandrem	14,719	12,387	84.15	12,232	82.32	7,993	68	3,767	32
Pernem	11,516	10,786	93.66	8,741	75.90	5,965	72	2,304	28
Siolim	12,909	7,282	56.41	11,681	90.48	5,583	49	5,868	51
Calangute	14,341	6,516	45.43	13,280	92.60	4,928	38	8,146	62
Aldona	12,902	5,963	46.29	12,472	96.66	4,700	38	7,609	62
Mapusa	12,872	8,398	65.70	11,900	93.09	5,859	49.87	5,889	50.13
Tivim	11,714	9,200	78.53	9,930	84.77	6,110	63	3,526	37
Bicholim	11,473	10,742	93.62	10,242	89.27	7,741	78	2,183	22
Pale	12,504	11,460	91.65	9,394	75.12	6,305	62	3,668	48
Satari	12,640	11,855	93.78	9,475	74.96	4,974	53	4,505	47
Panjim	11,137	6,931	62.23	10,502	94.29	4,175	40	6,245	60
St Cruz	13,971	5,756	41.19	13,132	94.00	4,311	33	8,609	66
St Andre	12,708	4,968	39.09	11,803	92.87	3,930	34	7,590	66
St Estevam	13,717	8,878	64.72	11,719	85.43	6,903	60	4,628	40
Marcaim	10,824	10,621	98.12	10,308	95.23	8,408	83	1,671	17
Ponda	11,874	10,383	89.12	11,395	95.96	8,082	72	3,090	28
Siroda	12,900	10,244	79.41	10,977	85.09	6,369	60	4,165	40
Sanguem	12,639	9,111	72.08	9,525	75.36	4,560	50	4,566	50
Canacona	13,540	9,855	72.78	10,764	79.49	5,832	56	4,622	44
Quepem	9,015	5,327	59.09	7,966	88.36	3,447	45	4,217	55
Curchorem	12,724	6,674	52.45	10,488	82.42	3,425	33	6,856	67

Continued

Constituency	No. of Voters	No. of Hindu Voters	%	Turn-out	%	Merger Vote	%	Union Territory Vote	%
Cuncolim	12,524	3,662	29.23	11,004	87.86	1,774	16	9,080	84
Benaulim	13,661	953	6.97	11,485	84.07	629	6	10,769	94
Navelim	15,775	4,059	25.73	13,575	86.05	3,061	23	10,335	77
Margao	12,603	5,633	44.69	10,503	83.33	3,241	30	7,157	70
Cortorim	16,776	1,001	5.96	13,746	81.93	926	6.8	12,597	91.50
Cortalim	13,597	1,887	13.87	11,962	87.97	1,376	11.68	10,411	88.32
Marmagao	21,773	16,123	73.50	16,000	73.48	7,654	48.64	8,072	51.32

Source: Adapted from Amonkar et al. n.d. *Goa Opinion Poll, Analytical Study of Voting Pattern*. Bastora.

Table 3
Lok Sabha Election Outcomes

North Constituency	Year	South Constituency
MGP	1963	MGP
MGP	1967	UGP
INC	1971	UGP
MGP	1977	INC
MGP	1980	INC
INC	1984	INC
MGP	1989	INC
INC	1991	INC
MGP	1996	UGDP
INC	1998	INC

Table 4
Detailed North (Panaji) Results

Year	Electors	Turnout %	No. of Candidates	Winner	Name	Runner-up	Third Party
1998	386,515	62	4	INC 27.9%	R. Naik	BJP 27.72%	MGP 21.4%
1996	386,000	55.9	9	MG 43.4%	R. Khalap	INC 38.4%	BJP 16.9%
1991	345,000	44.8	15	INC 58.2%	Harish Zantyre	MG 20.3%	BJP 17.8%
1989	333,000	73.8	13	MG 48.7%	Gopal Mayekar	INC 42.1%	
1984	291,000	73.1	12	INC 43%	S.L. Naik	MG 23.7%	
1980	262,000	71.9	5	MG 38.9%	S. Rane	INC 23.7%	
1977	243,000	63.6	6	MG 44.3%	Amrut Kansar	INC 37%	BLD 15.7%
1971	209,000	58.9	7	INC 48.3%	P. Kakodkar	MG 45.7%	
1967	202,000	71.8	8	MG 40.6%	J.J. Shinkre	UG 32.8%	INC 10.9%

Source: Butler et al. 1995: 172; *Lok Sabha Elections Handbook 1996.*

Table 5

Detailed South (Mormugao) Results

Year	Electors	Turnout %	No. of Candidates	Winner	Name	Runner-up	Third Party
1998	484,284	60.4	8	INC 30.46%	F. Sardinha	BJP 29.7%	UGDP 27.89%
1996	482,000	56	21	UGDP 40.5%	C. Alemao	INC 31.1%	BJP 13.7%
1991	409,000	40.3	18	INC 57.2%	E. Faleiro	MG 20.8%	BJP 13.6%
1989	400,000	45.1	12	INC 54.6%	E. Faleiro	JD 42.3%	
1984	296,000	70.5	9	INC 49.5%	E. Faleiro	GC 20.5%	MG 16.9%
1980	261,000	67.1	8	INC (U) 57%	E. Faleiro	MG 33%	JP 4.4
1977	234,000	62	9	INC 43.2%	E. Faleiro	MG 36.5%	BLD 13.6%
1971	226,000	53.1	6	UG 50.1%	E. de Sequeria	IND 37.9%	
1967	217,000	65.2	8	UG 39.4%	E. de Sequeira	IND 37.5%	

Source: et al. 1995: 172; *Lok Sabha Elections Handbook 1996*.

Appendix II

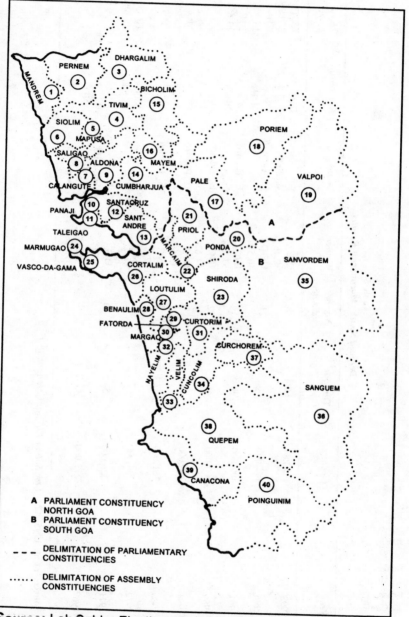

Bibliography

◆

Afonso, John Corriea. 1995. 'The Goan Christian Heritage.' In Narendra K. Wagle and George Coehlo, eds, *Goa: Continuity and Change*. Toronto: Centre for South Asian Studies of the University of Toronto, pp 1–12.

Ake, Claude. 1967. *A Theory of Political Integration*. Homewood, Illinois: The Dorsey Press.

Amonkar, Suresh G., Pundalik D. Gaitonde, Enfemiano Dias, Gurudas Duclo and Mohan Tamba. n.d. *Goa Opinion Poll, Analytical Study of Voting Pattern*. Bastora.

Anderson, Benedict R. O'G. 1983. *Imagined Communities: Reflections on the Origins and Spread of Nationalism*. London: Verso and NLB.

Anderson, Charles W., Fred R. Von der Mehden and Crawford Young. 1974. *Issues in Political Development*. Englewood Cliffs, N.J.: Prentice-Hall.

Angle, Prabhakar S. 1983. *Goa: An Economic Review*. Bombay: Goa Hindu Association Kala Vishag.

Bains, J.S. 1962. *India's International Disputes—A Legal Study*. Bombay: Asia Publishing House.

Barnett, Marguerite Ross. 1976. *The Politics of Cultural Nationalism in South India*. Princeton: Princeton University Press.

Barry, Brian. 1975a. 'The Consociational Model and Its Dangers,' *European Journal of Political Research* 3: 393–412.

Basu, Amrita. 1997. 'Reflections on Community Conflicts and the State in India,' *Journal of Asian Studies* 56: 391–97.

—————. 1975b. 'Political Accommodation and Consociational Democracy,' *British Journal of Political Science* 5: 476–505.

Bhargava, G.S. 1955. 'Behind India's Struggle for Goa,' *New Leader* 37 (September 12): 6–9.

Binder, Leonard. 1964. 'National Integration and Political Development,' *American Political Science Review* 58: 622–31.

Birch, Anthony. 1978. 'Minority Nationalist Movements and Theories of Political Integration,' *World Politics* 30: 325–44.

Boxer, Charles R. 1969. *The Portuguese Seaborne Empire, 1815–1825*. London: Weidenfeld and Nicholson.

Brass, Paul R. 1974. *Language, Religion and Politics in North India*. London: Cambridge University Press.

Brass, Paul R. 1975. 'Ethnic Cleavages and the Punjab Party System 1952–1972.' In Myron Weiner and John Osgood Field, eds, *Electoral Politics in the Indian States*, Vol. IV: *Party Systems and Cleavages*. Delhi: Manohar Book Service for the Massachusetts Institute of Technology Center for International Studies, pp 7–69.

—————. 1976. 'Ethnicity and Nationality Formation,' *Ethnicity* 3: 225–41.

—————. 1985. *Ethnic Groups and the State*. London: Croom Helm.

—————. 1991. *Ethnicity and Nationalism*. New Delhi: Sage Publications.

—————. 1994. *The Politics of India Since Independence*. 2nd ed. rev. Cambridge: Cambridge University Press.

—————. ed. 1996. *Riots and Pogroms*. New York: New York University Press.

—————. 1997. *Theft of an Idol: Text and Context in the Representation of Collective Violence.* Princeton: Princeton University Press.

Brecher, Michael. 1968. *India and World Politics, Krishna Menon's View of the World*. London: Oxford University Press.

Brown, W. Norman. 1972. *The United States and India, Pakistan, Bangladesh*. 3rd ed. rev. Cambridge: Harvard University Press.

Butler, David, Ashok Lahiri and **Prannoy Roy.** 1995. *India Decides, Elections 1952–1995*. New Delhi: Books and Things.

Carvalho, L. Cotta. 1966. *Goa: The Anatomy of Merger Politics*. Delhi: Goa, Daman & Diu Territorial Congress Committee.

Case Concerning Right of Passage Over Indian Territory (Merits), I.C.J. Reports, p. 6 (International Court of Justice, Vol. I, April 12, 1960), The Hague.

Cassinelli, C.W. 1969. 'The National Community,' *Polity* 2: 14–31.

Chandra, Bipan. 1984. *Communalism in Modern India*. Delhi: Vikas.

Chandra, Satish, K.C. Pande and **P.C. Mathur,** eds, 1976. *Regionalism and National Integration*. Jaipur: Aalekh Publishers.

Chary, S.T. 1955. 'Last Chapter in Freedom Struggle,' *Economic Weekly* VII (August 27): 1036–43 and (September 3): 1064–65.

Chavan, Y.B. 1961. 'Forces of Liberation,' *Vital Speeches and Documents of the Day* 2 (November 1): 62–63.

Claude, Inis L. 1955. *National Minorities, An International Problem*. Cambridge: Harvard University Press.

Cohen, Anthony. 1985. *The Symbolic Construction of Community*. Chichester: Ellis Horwood Limited, and London: Tavistock Publications.

Coleman, James and **Carl G. Rosberg, Jr.** 1964. *Political Parties and National Integration in Tropical Africa*. Berkeley: University of California Press.

Congress Bulletin, 1954–1963.

Connor, Walker. 1967. 'Self-Determination: The New Phase,'*World Politics* 20: 30–53.

—————. 1972. 'Nation Building or Nation Destroying?,' *World Politics* 24: 319–55.

—————. 1973. 'The Politics of Ethnonationalism,' *Journal of International Affairs* 27: 1–21.

—————. 1994. *Ethnonationalism, The Quest for Understanding*. Princeton: Princeton University Press.

Cooper, Randolf G.S. 1995. 'The Origin of the British Occupation of Goa.' In Narendra K. Wagle and George Coehlo, eds, *Goa: Continuity and Change*. Toronto: Centre for South Asian Studies of the University of Toronto, pp 146–64.

Cunha, T.B. 1957. 'Vatican is Against India on Goa,' *Organizer* 10 (May 27): 7, 14.
──────. 1958. 'Portuguese Imperialism and Indian Business,' *Vigil* 9 (August 23): 473–75.
──────. 1961. *Goa's Freedom Struggle*. Bombay: The T.B. Cunha Memorial Committee.
Daalder, Hans. 1974. 'The Consociational Democracy Theme,' *World Politics* 24: 604–21.
Dahl, Robert A. 1971. *Polyarchy, Participation and Opposition*. New Haven: Yale University Press.
Danvers, Frederick Charles. 1894. *The Portuguese in India*, 2 Vols. London: W.H. Allen & Co. Limited.
Das Gupta, Jyotirindra. 1968. 'Language Diversity and National Development.' In Joshua A. Fishman Charles A. Ferguson and Jyotirindra Das Gupta, eds, *Language Problems of Developing Nations*. New York: John Wiley & Sons, pp 17–26.
──────. 1970. *Language, Conflict and National Development*. Berkeley: University of California Press.
──────. 1997. 'Community, Authenticity, and Autonomy: Insurgence and Institutional Development in India's Northeast,' *Journal of Asian Studies* 56: 345–70.
Deora, M.S. 1995. *Liberation of Goa, Daman and Diu from Portuguese Rule*, Afro-Asian Liberation Movement Series. New Delhi: Discovery Press.
Deutsch, Karl. 1953a. 'The Growth of Nations: Some Recurrent Patterns of Political and Social Integration,' *World Politics* 5: 168–95.
──────. 1953b. *Nationalism and Social Communication*. Cambridge, Ma.: The M.I.T. Press.
──────. 1961. 'Social Mobilization and Political Development,' *American Political Science Review* 55: 493–514.
D'Souza, Bento Graciano. 1975. *Goan Society in Transition*. Bombay: Popular Prakashan.
deSouza, Peter Ronald. 1996a. 'A Democratic Verdict,' *Economic and Political Weekly* (January 13–20): 149–52.
──────. 1996b. 'The Accountability Factor,' *Seminar*, no. 440 (April): 36–39.
──────. 1996c. 'Community Factor Matters,' *Frontline* 13 (April 19): 46–47.
──────. 1996d. 'Goa: A Vote against Misgovernance,' *Frontline* 13 (June 14): 100–101.
Economist, 1955–1962.
Elder, Joseph W. 1964. 'National Loyalties in a Newly Independent Nation.' In David E. Apter, ed., *Ideology and Discontent*. New York: The Free Press, pp 77–92.
Enloe, Cynthia. 1973. *Ethnic Conflict and Political Development*. Boston: Little Brown.
Esman, Milton. 1973. 'The Management of Communal Conflict,' *Public Policy* 21: 49–78.
──────. 1977. *Ethnic Conflict in the Western World*. Ithaca: Cornell University Press.
Esteves, Sarto. 1966. *Goa and Its Future*. Bombay: Manaktalas.
──────. 1971. 'Growth of Political Leadership in Goa.' Unpublished Ph.D. dissertation, Department of Civics and Politics, University of Bombay.
──────. 1972. 'Parties and Politics in 1972 Assembly Elections in Goa.' *Political Science Review* 11: 138–53.
──────. 1976. 'Goa, Daman and Diu.' In Iqbal Narain, ed., *State Politics in India*. New Delhi: Meenakshi Prakashan, pp 477–505.

Esteves, Sarto. 1986. *Politics and Political Leadership in Goa.* New Delhi: Sterling Publishers Private Ltd.

Etzioni, Amitai. 1993. *The Spirit of Community.* New York: Touchstone Books.

Fera, Ivan. 1987. 'The Tempest,' *Illustrated Weekly of India*(January 11): pp 32–35.

Fernandes, Aureliano. 1997. *Cabinet Government in Goa.* Panaji: Maureen & Canvet Pub.

Fisher, Margaret W. 1962. 'Goa in Wider Perspective,' *Asian Survey* 2: 3–10.

Foreign Affairs Record, 1954–1962. India, Ministry of External Affairs.

Foreign Affairs Reports, 1954–1962.

Frankel, Francine. 1978. *India's Political Economy, 1947–77.* Princeton: Princeton University Press.

Gaitonde, Pundalik. 1987. *The Liberation of Goa, A Participant's View of History.* London: C. Hurst and Co.

Gaitonde, Pundalik and **A.D. Mani.** 1956. *The Goa Problem.* New Delhi: Indian Council for World Affairs.

Galbraith, John Kenneth. 1969. *Ambassador's Journal.* Boston: Houghton-Mifflin Company.

Geertz, Clifford. 1963. *Old Societies and New States.* New York: The Free Press.

Glasgow, George. 1954. 'The Case of Goa,' *Contemporary Review* 186: 249–50.

'Goa and India,' 1965. Editorial, *Modern Review* 118 (August): 89–90.

Goa Chamber of Commerce & Industry. 1992. *Thirty Years of Economic Development in Goa 1961–1991.* Panjim.

Goa Petitioners in the United Nations. 1964. Goa Freedom Movement Publication.

Goa Today, 1965–1998.

[Gomantaki]. 1957. 'Goa and India and the World,' *Mankind* 2 (October): 197–211.

Gomantak Times, 1994–1998.

Gopal, Sarvepalli. 1979. *Jawaharlal Nehru, A Biography*, Vol. II: *1947–1956.* Delhi: Oxford University Press.

—————. 1984. *Jawaharlal Nehru, A Biography*, Vol. III: *1956–1964.* London: Jonathan Cape.

Gorwala, A.D. 1961. 'The Goa Affair,' *Janata* 16 (31 December): 15–16.

Government of Goa. *Assembly Elections Ready Reference.* 1994. Panaji: Department of Information and Publicity, Government of Goa.

—————. *Official Gazette*, 1967–1987.

—————. *Lok Sabha Elections Reference Handbook.* 1996. Panaji: Department of Information and Publicity.

Gune, V.T., ed. 1979. *Gazetteer of the Union Territory of Goa, Daman and Diu.* District Gazetteer Part I: *Goa.* Panaji: Gazetteer Department, Government of the Union Territory of Goa, Daman and Diu.

Gupta, Anand. 1962. *Friend or Foe? USA Unmasked in Goa.* New Delhi: New Literature.

Haas, Ernest B. 1968. *The Uniting of Europe.* Stanford: Stanford University Press.

Hah, Chong-Do and **Jeffrey Martin.** 1975. 'Towards a Synthesis of Conflict and Integration Theories of Nationalism,' *World Politics* 24: 361–86.

Halappa, G.S., K. Raghavendra Rao and **A.M. Rajaskhariah.** 1964. *The First General Elections in Goa.* Dharwar: Karnatak University Press.

Hardgrave, Robert L., Jr. 1965. *The Dravidian Movement.* Bombay: Popular Prakashan.

Hardgrave, Robert L., Jr. 1970. *India, Government and Politics in a Developing Nation*. New York: Harcourt, Brace and World.

—————. 1993. 'The Challenge of Ethnic Conflict in India: The Dilemmas of Diversity,' *Journal of Democracy* 4: 54–68.

Harrison, Selig S. 1956. 'The Challenge to Indian Nationalism,' *Foreign Affairs* 34: 620–36.

—————. 1960. *India—The Most Dangerous Decades*. Princeton: Princeton University Press.

Herald, 1991–1998.

Higgs, David. 1995. 'The Inquisition in Late Eighteenth Century Goa.' In Narendra K. Wagle and George Coehlo, eds, *Goa: Continuity and Change*. Toronto: Centre for South Asian Studies of the University of Toronto, pp 123–45.

Hindu (Madras), 1961–1996.

Hindustan Overseas Times (New Delhi), 1954–1955.

Hindustan Times (New Delhi), 1961–1996.

Historical Society of the Foreign Office. 1920. *Portuguese Possessions in India*. Handbook No. 79. London: H.M. Stationary Office.

Horowitz, Donald L. 1971. 'Three Dimensions of Ethnic Politics,' *World Politics* 20: 239–44.

—————. 1985. *Ethnic Groups in Conflict*. Berkeley: University of California Press.

Huntington, Samuel. 1968. *Political Order in Changing Societies*. New Haven: Yale University Press.

Information Service of India. n.d. *The Story of Goa*. London.

India News Network Digest. 1993–1998. India-D Editor <editor[arf]indnet.org>

India, *Lok Sabha Debates*, 1952–1996.

India, *Rajya Sabha Debates*, 1952–1996.

India Abroad, 1991–1996.

India Today, 1987–1997.

Indian Embassy. 1961. *The Prime Minister Comes to America*. Washington: Indian Embassy.

Indian Institute of Public Opinion. *Monthly Public Opinion Survey,* October–November 1962.

Jacob, Philip E. and **James V. Toscano.** 1964. *The Integration of Political Communities*. Philadelphia and New York: J.B. Lippincott Company.

Jaffrelot, Christophe. 1996. *The Hindu Nationalist Movement in India*. New York: Columbia University Press.

Joshi, Ram. 1964. 'The General Elections in Goa,' *Asian Survey* 4: 1093–1101.

Kahane, Reuven. 1982. *Legitimacy and Integration in Developing Societies: The Case of India*. Boulder: Westview Press.

Kahin, George Mc Turnan. 1956. *The Asian-African Conference*. Ithaca, N.Y.: Cornell University Press.

Kasfir, Nelson. 1979. 'Explaining Ethnic Political Participation,' *World Politics* 31: 365–88.

Kavic, Lorne J. 1967. *India's Quest for Security*. Berkeley and Los Angeles: University of California Press.

Keesing's Contemporary Archives, 1955–1962.

Keyes, Charles F. 1981. *Ethnic Change.* Seattle: University of Washington Press.

Khera, P.N. 1974. *Operation Vijay, The Liberation of Goa and Other Portuguese Colonies in India.* New Delhi: Historical Section, Ministry of Defence, Government of India.

Kochanek, Stanley A. 1968. *The Congress Party of India.* Princeton: Princeton University Press.

Kohli, Atul. 1990. 'From Majority to Minority Rule.' In Marshall Bouton and Philip Oldenburg, eds, *India Briefing, 1990.* Boulder: Westview Press, pp 1–23.

————. 1997. 'Can Democracies Accommodate Ethnic Nationalism? Rise and Decline of Self-Determination Movements in India,' *Journal of Asian Studies* 56: 325–44.

Kosambi, D.D. 1962. *Myth and Reality.* Bombay: Popular Prakashan.

Kothari, Rajni. 1964. 'The Congress System in India,' *Asian Survey* 4: 1161–73.

Kulkarni, Vinayak. 1956. *Latest Struggle for Goa.* Socialist Tract No. 3. Hyderabad: Socialist Party.

Kunte, D.G. ed. 1978. *Goa Freedom Struggle vis-a-vis Maharashtra.* Vol. VIII: Two Parts. Bombay: Gazetteers Department, Government of Maharashtra.

Lach, Donald F. 1968. *India in the Eyes of Europe: The Sixteenth Century.* Chicago: Phoenix Books, The University of Chicago Press.

Lambert, Richard D. 1977. 'Ethnic Conflict in the Modern World Today,' *The Annals of the American Academy of Political and Social Sciences*, no. 433 (September), preface.

LaPalombara, Joseph E. and **Myron Weiner,** eds, 1966. *Political Parties and Political Development.* Princeton, N.J.: Princeton University Press.

Legislative Assembly of Goa, Daman and Diu Debates, 1965–1987.

Lijphart, Arend. 1968. *The Politics of Accommodation.* Berkeley: University of California Press.

————. 1969. 'Consociational Democracy,' *World Politics* 21 January: 207–25.

————. 1971. 'Cultural Diversity and Theories of Political Integration,' *Canadian Journal of Political Science* 4: 1–14.

————. 1977. *Democracy in Plural Societies, A Comparative Exploration.* New Haven: Yale University Press.

————. 1996. 'The Puzzle of Indian Democracy: A Consociational Interpretation,' *American Political Science Review* 90: 258–68.

Link, 1961.

Lipset, Seymour Martin. 1963. *Political Man.* Garden City: Anchor Books.

Lobo, Crescencio. 1927. *Portuguese India: Its Commerce and Industries.* Bombay: Times Press.

Lok Sabha Secretariat. 1966. *Foreign Policy of India, Texts of Documents 1947–1964.* New Delhi.

Lorwin, Val R. 1971. 'Segmented Pluralism: Ideological Cleavages and Political Cohesion in the Smaller European Democracies,' *Comparative Politics* 3: 141–76.

Lustick, Ian. 1979. 'Stability in Deeply Divided Societies: Consociationalism versus Control,' *World Politics* 31: 325–45.

Mankekar, D.R. 1962. *The Goa Action.* Bombay: Popular Book Depot.

Manor, James. 1982. 'The Dynamics of Political Integration and Disintegration.' In A.J. Wilson and Dennis Dalton, eds, *The States of South Asia, Problems of National Integration.* London: C. Hurst & Co., pp 89–110.

Mascarenhas-Keyes, Stella. 1989. 'International Migration: Its Economic Impact on Goa up to 1961.' In Teotonio R. de Souza, ed., *Goa Through the Ages*, vol. II. New Delhi: Concept Publishing Company, pp 242–62.

Mason, Anthony. ed. 1967. *India and Ceylon: Unity and Diversity*. London: Oxford University Press.

Mazuri, Ali. 1969. 'Pluralism and National Integration.' In Leo Kuper and M.G. Smith, eds, *Pluralism in Africa*. Berkeley: University of California Press, pp 330–50.

McCrae, Kenneth D. 1974. *Consociational Democracy*. The Carleton Library, No. 79. Toronto: McClelland and Stewart Ltd.

Melson, Robert and **Howard Wolpe.** 1970. 'Modernization and the Politics of Communalism: A Comparative Perspective,' *American Political Science Review* 64: 1112–50.

Menon, V.P. 1961. *The Story of the Integration of the Indian States*. Calcutta: Orient Longman Private Ltd.

Miles, William F.S. 1995. *Imperial Burdens, Countercolonialism in Former French India*. Boulder: Lynne Rienner Publishers.

Ministry of Information and Broadcasting. 1961. *National Integration*. New Delhi: Ministry of Information and Broadcasting.

Mitra, Subrata K. and **R. Alison Lewis.** 1996. *Subnational Movements in South Asia*. Boulder: Westview Press.

Mohan, M. Madan. 1996. 'Congress I Drubbed in Goa,' *Frontline* 13 (May 31): 130–31.

Montemayor, J.M. 1970. 'A Sociological Analysis of a Goan Village Community.' Unpublished Ph.D. dissertation, Department of Sociology, University of Delhi.

Moraes, Frank. 1956. *Jawaharlal Nehru: A Biography*. New York: The Macmillan Company.

Moraes, George Mark. 1964. *A History of Christianity in India*. Bombay: Manaktalas.

Morris-Jones, W.H. 1954. 'Portuguese Pockets,' *New Statesman* 48 (July 24): 96.

Morrison, Donald G. and **Hugh Michael Stevenson.** 1972a. 'Cultural Pluralism, Modernization, and Conflict,' *Canadian Journal of Political Science* 5: 82–103.

——————. 1972b. 'Integration and Instability,' *American Political Science Review* 66: 902–27.

'Mr Nehru's Adventure.' 1961. *Spectator* (December 22): 920.

Narain, Iqbal. 1976. 'Cultural Pluralism, National Integration and Democracy in India,' *Asian Survey* 16: 903–17.

National Council of Applied Economic Research. 1964. *Techno-Economic Survey of Goa, Daman and Diu*. New Delhi.

——————. 1970. *Development Programmes for Goa, Daman and Diu*. New Delhi.

National Secretariat for Information. 1962. *The Invasion and Occupation of Goa in the World Press*. Lisbon.

NATO Information Service. 1965. *Facts About the North Atlantic Treaty Organization*. Paris.

Navhind Times. 1963–1998.

Nayar, Baldev Raj. 1966. *Minority Politics in the Punjab*. Princeton: Princeton University Press.

Nehru, B.K. 1962. 'Goa.' Address before the Harvard and Radcliffe Clubs of Washington, D.C., January 24.

Nehru, Jawaharlal. 1956. *The Goa Question*. New Delhi: Ministry of External Affairs.

—————. 1958a. *Speeches, August 1949–February 1953*. New Delhi: Publications Division, Ministry of Information and Broadcasting, Government of India.

—————. 1958b. *Speeches, March 1953–August 1957*. New Delhi: Publications Division, Ministry of Information and Broadcasting, Government of India.

—————. 1964. *Speeches, September 1957–April 1963*. New Delhi: Publications Division, Ministry of Information and Broadcasting, Government of India.

—————. 1968. *Speeches, March 1963–May 1964*. New Delhi: Publications Division, Ministry of Information and Broadcasting, Government of India.

New Age, 1955–1962.

Newman, Robert S. 1981. 'Green Revolution, Blue Revolution: The Predicament of India's Traditional Fishermen,' *South Asia* 4: 35–46.

—————. 1984. 'Goa: The Transformation of an Indian Region,' *Pacific Affairs* 47: 420–49.

—————. 1988. 'Konkani Mai Ascends the Throne: The Cultural Basis of Goan Statehood,' *South Asia* 11: 1–24.

New York Times, 1946–1997.

Nordlinger, Eric. 1972. *Conflict Regulation in Divided Societies*. Cambridge: Harvard University Center for International Affairs, Occasional Paper No. 29.

Organizer, 1961.

Overstreet, Gene D. and **Marshall Windmiller.** 1959. *Communalism in India*. Berkeley: University of California Press.

Pai Panandiker, V.A. and **P.N. Chaudhuri.** 1983. *Demographic Transition in Goa and Its Policy Implications*. New Delhi: Uppal Publishing House under the auspices of the Centre for Policy Research.

Palmer, W. Norman. 1958. 'Indian Attitudes toward Colonialism.' In Robert Strausz-Hupe and Harry W. Hazard, eds, *The Idea of Colonialism*. New York: Frederick A. Praeger, pp 271–310.

—————. 1963. 'The 1962 Election in North Bombay,' *Pacific Affairs* 36: 120–37.

Pandey, Gyanendra. 1990. *The Construction of Communalism in North India*. Delhi: Oxford University Press.

—————. ed. 1993. *Hindus and Others*. New Delhi: Viking.

Parker, R.H. 1955. 'The French and Portuguese Settlements in India,' *Political Quarterly* 26: 389–98.

Parthasarathi, G. ed. 1986. *Jawaharlal Nehru, Letters to Chief Ministers*, Vol. 2: *1950–1952*. London: Oxford University Press for the Jawaharlal Nehru Memorial Fund.

—————. 1988. *Jawaharlal Nehru, Letters to Chief Ministers*, Vol. 4: *1954–1957*. London: Oxford University Press for the Jawaharlal Nehru Memorial Fund.

Pattee, Richard. 1957. *Portugal and the Portuguese of the Orient*. Milwaukee: The Bruce Publishing Company.

Pearson, M.N. 1987. *The New Cambridge History of India, Vol. I: The Portuguese in India*. Cambridge: Cambridge University Press.

Phadnis, Urmila. 1989. *Ethnicity and Nation-building in South Asia*. New Delhi: Sage Publications.

Pinto, J.B. 1962. *Goan Emigration.* Saligao: Privately Printed.

Pisurlekar, Pandurang S. 1975. *The Portuguese and the Marathas.* Trans. P.R. Kakodkar. Bombay: State Board for Literature and Culture, Government of Maharashtra.

Poplai, S.L. ed. 1959. *Selected Documents on Asian Affairs, India 1947–50,* Vol. II: *External Affairs.* London: Oxford University Press.

'*Portugal's Intervention in Goa.*' 1957. *United Nations Review* 4 (November): 107.

Priolkar, A.K. 1961. *The Goa Inquisition.* Bombay: Bombay University Press.

——————. 1967. *Goa Rediscovered.* Bombay: Bhaktal Books Intl.

Raghaven, G.N.S. 1956. 'Predicament in Goa,' *Encounter* 6: 62–64.

Rajagopalachari, C. 1961–62. 'Dear Reader,' *Swarajya* 6 (December 30): 9–10 and (January 6): 11.

Rajan, M.S. 1960–61. 'Stresses and Strains in Indo-British Relations 1954–56,' *International Studies* 2: 153–89.

——————. 1967. *India in World Affairs 1954–1966.* Bombay: Asia Publishing House.

Rajkumar, N.V. 1951. *The Problem of French India.* New Delhi: All India Congress Committee.

——————. ed. 1957. *The Background of India's Foreign Policy.* Delhi: Indian National Congress.

Rao, K. Narayana. 1956. 'The Problem of Goa,' *Indian Yearbook of International Affairs* 5: 61–67.

Rao, P.K. 1963. *Portuguese Rule in Goa.* Bombay: Asia Publishing House.

Rashtramat, 1970–1979.

[Remy]. 1957. *Goa—Rome of the Orient.* Trans. Lancelot C. Sheppard. London: Arthur Barker Ltd.

Report of the States Reorganization Commission. 1955. New Delhi: Government of India Press.

Rev. Mons. Sebastiao Xavier dos Remedios Monteiro v State, AIR 1968 Goa, Daman and Diu 17 (v. 55 C6).

Ribeiro, Dioniso A. 1966. 'Emotional Integration of Goans.' In A.B. Shah, ed., *Goa: The Problems of Transition.* Bombay: Manaktalas, pp 73–88.

Rothchild, Donald. 1970. 'Ethnicity and Conflict Resolution,' *World Politics* 22: 597–616.

Rothchild, Joseph. 1981. *Ethnopolitics: A Conceptual Framework.* New York: Columbia University Press.

Rubinoff, Arthur G. 1971. *India's Use of Force in Goa.* Bombay: Popular Prakashan.

——————. 1980. 'The Change of Government in Goa—The Emergence of Issue Politics in a Communal Setting.' Paper presented to the Canadian Asian Studies Association, Montreal, Quebec, May 26.

——————. 1983. 'Integration Theories and the Case of Goa.' In Milton Israel, ed., *National Unity: The South Asian Experience.* New Delhi: Promilla & Co., pp 165–208.

——————. 1991. 'The Multilateral Imperative in India's Foreign Policy,' *The Roundtable,* no. 319: 313–34.

——————. 1992. 'Goa's Attainment of Statehood,' *Asian Survey* 32: 471–87.

——————. 1995a. 'Goa's Campaign for Statehood.' In Narendra K. Wagle and George Coehlo, eds, *Goa: Continuity and Change.* Toronto: Centre for South Asian Studies of the University of Toronto, pp 73–93.

Rubinoff, Arthur G. 1995b. 'Political Integration in Goa,' *Journal of Developing Societies* 11: 36–60.

──────. 1997a. 'National Identity in Goa.' In Reeta Chowdhari Tremblay, ed., *Perspectives on South Asia at the Threshold of the 21st Century*. Montreal: Canadian Association of South Asian Studies.

──────. 1997b. 'The Defeat of Eduardo Faleiro: South Goa Parliamentary Election,' *Economic and Political Weekly*, 39 (September 27): 2469–72.

Rubinoff, Janet A. 1992. 'Casta and Communidade: The Transformation of Corporate Agrarian Structures in Goa, India.' Unpublished Ph.D. dissertation, Department of Anthropology, University of Toronto.

──────. 1995. 'The Casteing of Catholicism: Goan Responses to Conversion.' In Narendra K. Wagle and George Coehlo, eds, *Goa: Continuity and Change*. Toronto: Centre for South Asian Studies of the University of Toronto, pp 165–81.

Rudolph, Lloyd I. and **Susanne H.** 1967. *The Modernity of Tradition*. Chicago: University of Chicago Press.

Saksena, R.N. 1974. *Goa into the Mainstream*. New Delhi: Abhinav Publications.

Salazar, Oliveira. 1956. 'Goa and the Indian Union—The Portuguese View,' *Foreign Affairs* 24: 418–31.

──────. 1962. '*The Invasion and Occupation of Goa by the Indian Union,*' Speech to the National Assembly, January 3, 1962. Lisbon: Secretariado da Information.

Saldana, C.F. 1957. *A Short History of Goa*. Goa: Impresna Nacional.

Sardesai, S.G. 1953. *Forward to the Liberation of Goa*. New Delhi: New Age Press.

Schermerhorn, R.A. 1978. *Ethnic Plurality in India*. Tucson: University of Arizona Press.

Schlesinger, Arthur M., Jr. 1965. *A Thousand Days*. Boston: Houghton Mifflin Company.

Scholberg, Henry. 1982. *Bibliography of Goa and the Portuguese in India*. New Delhi: Promilla & Co.

Scott, Robert E. 1966. 'Political Parties and Policy Making in Latin America.' In Joseph E. LaPalombara and Myron Weiner, eds, *Political Parties and Political Development*. Princeton, N.J.: Princeton University Press, pp 331–67.

Shadi, Zilpha Tedfora. 1962. 'Goa: A Case Study of the Formation of Indian Foreign Policy.' Unpublished Master's dissertation, Department of Political Science, University of California.

Sharma, Suresh K. 1968. *Union Territory Administration in India*. Chandigarh: Chandi Publications.

Singh, Jaswant. ed. 1962. *Indian Armed Forces Yearbook 1961–1962*. Bombay.

Smith, Anthony. 1971. *Theories of Nationalism*. London: Duckworth.

──────. 1981. *The Ethnic Revival in the Modern World*. Cambridge: Cambridge University Press.

──────. 1991. *National Identity*. Reno: University of Nevada Press.

──────. 1993. 'The Ethnic Sources of Nationalism,' *Survival* 35: 48–62.

──────. 1995. *Nations and Nationalism in a Global Era*. Cambridge: Polity Press.

Soares, Elevterio. 1955. 'Goa's Liberation: Prospects and Possibilities,' *Modern Review* 98: 453–55.

Srinivas, M.N. 1976. *Nation-Building in Independent India*. Delhi: Oxford University Press.

State Department Central Files, National Archives, Washington, D.C. 1946–1963.
Statesman, 1961–1996.
Statesman Weekly, 1969–1980.
Stokes, Gale. 1978. 'The Underdeveloped Theory of Nationalism,' *World Politics*
    31: 150–60.
Stern, Robert W. 1970. *The Process of Opposition in India*. Chicago: University of
    Chicago Press.
Streiff, Eric. 1955. 'Test Case Goa,' *Swiss Review of World Affairs* 5: 4.
Study Team on Administration of Union Territories and NEFA. 1968. *Report*. New
    Delhi: Administrative Reforms Commission.
Subrahmanyam, Sanjay. 1993. *The Portuguese Empire in Asia, 1500–1700*. New
    York: Longman Publishing.
Tambiah, Stanley J. 1996. *Levelling Crowds, Ethnonationalist Conflict in South
    Asia*. Berkeley: University of California Press.
Taylor, David. 1979. 'Political Identity In South Asia,' In David Taylor and
    Malcom Yapp, eds, *Political Identity in South Asia*. London: Curzon Press, pp
    255–65.
The Times of India (New Delhi), 1962–1996.
Tremblay, Reeta Chowdhari. 1997. 'Living Multiculturally in a Federal India.' In
    C. Steven La Rue, ed., *Regional Handbook of Economic Development: Vol. II:
    India: Prospects into the 21st Century*. Chicago: Fitzroy Dearborn Publishers,
    pp 158–69.
'*Treaty of Succession of the French Establishments of Pondicherry, Karaikal, Mahe
    and Yanam*,' 1956. *Indian Yearbook of International Affairs* 5: 175–88.
United Nations. 1960. *Demographic Yearbook*. New York: United Nations.
United Nations General Assembly. 1960 and 1961. Official Records, 947th and
    948th Meetings, December 14 and 15, 1960; and 1083rd Meeting, December 18,
    1961.
United Nations Security Council. 1961. Official Records, 987th and 988th Meetings,
    December 18, 1961.
U.S. Department of State. 1994. *Foreign Relations of the United States, 1961–1963*,
    Vol. XIII: *West Europe and Canada*. Washington: Government Printing Office.
U.S. Department of State Bulletin, 1955–1962.
van de Berghe, Pierre. 1969. 'Pluralism and the Polity: A Theoretical Exploration.'
    In Leo Kuper and M.G. Smith, eds, *Pluralism in Africa*. Berkeley: University
    of California Press, pp 67–81.
van den Helm, Robert P. 1974. 'Aspects of the Study of State Formation and
    Nation-Building,' *International Journal of Politics* 4: 3–39.
van der Veer, Peter. 1994. *Religious Nationalism*. Berkeley: University of California
    Press.
Van Hollen, Christopher. 1980. 'The Tilt Policy Revisited: Nixon-Kissinger Geo-
    politics and South Asia,' *Asian Survey* 20: 339–61.
Varshney, Ashutosh. 1993. 'Contested Meanings: India's National Identity, Hindu
    Nationalism, and the Politics of Anxiety,' *Daedalus* 122: 227–61.
Waldron, Arthur N. 1985. 'Theories of Nationalism and Historical Explanation,'
    World Politics 36: 416–33.
Weiner, Myron. 1965. 'Political Integration and Political Development,' *The Annals
    of the American Academy of Political and Social Sciences*, no. 358: 52–64.

Weiner, Myron. 1967. *Party Building in a New Nation*. Chicago: University of Chicago Press.

—————. ed. 1968. *State Politics in India*. Princeton: Princeton University Press.

—————. 1978. *Sons of the Soil, Migration and Ethnic Conflict in India*. Princeton: Princeton University Press.

Welsh, David. 1993. 'Domestic Conflict and Ethnic Conflict,' *Survival* 35: 63–80.

West Coast Times, 1979.

Whiteway, R.S. 1899. *The Rise of Portuguese Power in India 1497–1550*. Westminister: Archibald Constable & Co.

Young, Crawford. 1976. *The Politics of Cultural Pluralism*. Madison: The University of Wisconsin Press.

Zolberg, Aristide R. 1967. 'Patterns of National Integration,' *The Journal of Modern African Studies* 5: 449–67.

Zuckerman, Alan. 1975. 'Political Cleavages: A Conceptual and Theoretical Analysis,' *British Journal of Political Science* 5: 231–48.

Index

◆

About the Author

◆

Arthur G. Rubinoff is currently Professor at the Department of Political Science, University of Toronto, Canada. Over a long and distinguished career his research has been suppported by the Ford Foundation, the Fulbright Foundation, the Shastri Indo-Canadian Institute, the Smithsonian Institution and the Social Sciences and Humanities Research Council of Canada. A regular contributor to scholarly journals of repute, Professor Rubinoff is the author of *India's Use of Force in Goa*; the editor of *Canada and South Asia: Issues and Opportunities, Canada and the States of South Asia*, and *Canada and South Asia: Political and Strategic Relations*; and the co-editor of *International Conflict and Conflict Management*.